W9-BWZ-730

THE 4% FIX

THE

4%
FIX

HOW **ONE HOUR**
CAN CHANGE **YOUR LIFE**

KARMA BROWN

Collins

The 4% Fix
Copyright © 2020 by Karma Brown.
All rights reserved.

Published by Collins, an imprint of HarperCollins Publishers Ltd

First edition

No part of this book may be used or reproduced in any manner whatsoever without the prior written permission of the publisher, except in the case of brief quotations embodied in reviews.

HarperCollins books may be purchased for educational, business or sales promotional use through our Special Markets Department.

HarperCollins Publishers Ltd
Bay Adelaide Centre, East Tower
22 Adelaide Street West, 41st Floor
Toronto, Ontario, Canada
M5H 4E3

www.harpercollins.ca

Library and Archives Canada Cataloguing in Publication

Title: The 4% fix : how one hour can change your life / Karma Brown.
Other titles: 4 percent fix | Four percent fix | 4 per cent fix | Four per cent fix
Names: Brown, Karma, author.
Identifiers: Canadiana (print) 20200323148 | Canadiana (ebook) 2020032327X |
ISBN 9781443458627 (softcover) | ISBN 9781443458634 (ebook)
Subjects: LCSH: Time management. | LCSH: Self-management (Psychology) |
LCSH: Goal (Psychology)
Classification: LCC BF637.T5 B76 2020 | DDC 640/.43—dc23

Printed and bound in the United States of America

LSC/C 9 8 7 6 5 4 3 2 1

*To our daughter, who taught me (okay, forced me)
to "get up and get at it" at 5 a.m.*

I'm glad you sleep in now, even if I can't.

Lost time is never found again.
—BENJAMIN FRANKLIN

CONTENTS

INTRODUCTION: IT'S ABOUT TIME

Life seems but a quick succession of busy nothings.
—JANE AUSTEN, *MANSFIELD PARK*

A few months ago, my daughter and I were listening to a podcast about black holes. Along with interesting tidbits, like that black holes aren't actually holes at all (rather, a compressed mass of incredibly dense matter) and how they're created (a star explodes and caves in on itself, blocking out all light), what fascinated both of us was the notion of time in relation to these mysterious "holes." Specifically, the idea of time travel.

This concept was as captivating to an 11-year-old as it was to her significantly older mother, though for different reasons. We both imagined the wonder of it, and the fun of asking "Where would you go?" But secretly I also considered the practicality of it (how very "boring adult" of me). I mean, imagine *all the things you could do* if you weren't constrained by the time continuum? Of course, while many scientists believe time travel via black holes is possible *in theory*, no one can be sure exactly how it would work. Because even if you could find your way into a black hole, it's postulated that the immense gravitational force would simultaneously compress you horizontally and stretch you vertically—like a noodle—in a phenomenon aptly called "spaghettification." Yes, it really is called that.

We all have different relationships with time, and these seem to become more complex and angsty with every birthday candle we add to our cake. Overwhelmingly these days, it also feels as though many of us don't have enough of it. I remember, in my early days of being a mom, seeing a meme about how the days are long but the years are short. It had been posted in reference to parenthood—and it is wholly accurate in that context—but I have found it also applies to life in general. If we find ourselves racing through a "quick succession of busy nothings" day in, day out, we may also find ourselves, years down the road, wondering where all that time really went. What do we have to show for all that busyness?

I had my own rough patch with time about a decade ago. Only a few years earlier, if you'd told me that in the future I'd be waking most days at 5 a.m.—on purpose, without an alarm—I would have said, "You've got the wrong girl." I was a night owl, doing my best things and having my best times after 9 p.m. The only "morning people" I knew were either retired or under the age of five. Even though I didn't sleep in much past 8 a.m., even on weekends, 5 a.m. was still the *middle of the night* as far as I was concerned.

I wish I could tell you my transition from night owl to morning lark had been my own brilliant idea, fuelled by a desire to write my first novel and inspired by the sentiment "If not now, when?" I could lie and say I set my alarm diligently each night and went to bed early enough that waking at 4:45 a.m. didn't feel like the worst decision ever made. If I could rewrite history, I'd tell you that when my alarm blared, I peeled off the covers with vigour, flooded by motivation, rather than stumbling bleary-eyed down the staircase and weeping quietly until the coffee finished brewing.

Here's the truth about how I joined the early-risers club and got a handle on my current relationship with time: we became parents to a baby who didn't like to sleep. And when your kid hates sleeping, guess what? You don't get to sleep either. I joke that my daughter sleep-trained me rather than the other way around—she was a definitive morning-lark child (as many are) who never, ever, napped. As a toddler, she ran middle-of-the-night circles in the living room, singing along to Dora the Explorer while I lay on the couch, dazed and dog-tired, wondering where I went off course. Some mornings it was only 3 a.m. when the circus began. That was when she woke up. *For the day*.

Basically, I hated those painfully early mornings with a passion . . . until one day I didn't hate them so much. It was then that time and I came to an understanding: those hours were mine, and I could do with them what I wanted. Once I discovered the magic of writing early in the morning, I felt unstoppable. That pre-dawn hour was full of opportunity.

Nothing significant had happened yet to derail my day. Emails were not pinging holes into my focus. Social media was quieter, as the flurry of tweets and posts from the late-night crowd had become old news.

So I learned to focus bright and early alongside my daughter's television programs, the glue and glitter slinging from her 6 a.m. crafts often ending up spackled on my computer keys. Eventually I became skilled enough in our morning routine that I didn't have to break my writing stride to answer her constant peppering of questions, like "Would you rather be eaten by a shark or *be* the shark that eats people?"

We all have the same 24 hours in a day, 365 days a year. There is no way to turn back time or stop the clock—those seconds, minutes, hours . . . they tick along regardless. But while you can't actually manipulate time, *you can choose what you do with it*. It's worth noting—in case you're thinking this is not replicable—that literally anyone (yes, even you) can do this: I am not an outlier. I do not have short-sleep syndrome like people whose genes mean they only need a couple of hours of shut-eye nightly. I have no special skills or expertise for waking up early. It is simple, though admittedly not easy to do, and it begins with this question: *If I gave you one hour a day for something you've always wished to find time for—even if the "how" details were fuzzy—what would you do with it?*

To be clear, we're talking about a mere 4% of your day—one single hour. So what bakes your cake? Training for a 10K race or triathlon? Learning to play the guitar? Reading the stack of books that currently hold up your bedside table lamp? Have you ever longed to take up knitting, or painting, or cooking? Maybe you have a book in you, like I did. Perhaps you dream of speaking another language, if only you could find uninterrupted minutes to practise. Maybe you used to love playing the piano, but now it's a junk-mail holder and dust bunny catcher, and you wish you could get back to it. The goal of this book, therefore, and my hope in writing it, is to help you discover your own 4% time fix, and to offer a clear plan for making it part of your daily life. Because until we sort out this whole black-hole time-travel and "spaghettification" issue, we're stuck with the hours we have.

It's likely you could use this gifted hour to catch up on sleep, or clean out junk drawers, or tackle your bloated inbox. From one semi-sleep-deprived person with too many junk drawers and a messy inbox to another, *I hear that*. However, this 4% fix isn't about catching up or getting ahead of your day, even if you really love to sleep and really hate those unread mail flags. We're aiming higher here, friends. Because while we all have the same number of hours in a day, none of us knows exactly *how many* of those hours we're going to get in the end. And I plan to exploit the heck out of the ones I get.

But before we begin, a few ground rules:

1. **You do you.** "One size fits all" is generally a bad idea for most things in life (like nutrition, education, bathing suits . . .), and this approach is no different. I believe around 5 a.m. is the best time for a 4% fix, and there's even science on my side, but more on that later. However, I won't be there to drag you out of bed each morning. You need to

find your own groove (with a side of grit) to make this work.

2. **This hour is not about productivity.** It's not a race or a competition, nor is the goal to secure a slot on one of those "the world's most successful people rise with the sun" lists. The only person you are accountable to here is you (see ground rule #1).

3. **Be open.** Be willing to try anything once, including setting a very early morning alarm. This "be open" strategy is one I personally ascribe to, and as a result, over the years I have eaten curried mealworms, ziplined upside down, held a boa constrictor around my shoulders and a tarantula in my hand, and tried my first Pop-Tart (at the age of 43). Of all these things, the Pop-Tart was by far the most regrettable.

4. **Do the work.** Because no one else is going to do it for you.

Your first task? Set a 5 a.m. alarm for tomorrow morning. Do it right now.

Just kidding. That would be nuts, because much like distance running or hot sauce or forty-degree humidity or new shoes, it takes some time and exposure to acclimatize to the early-risers club. So your first task on the way to your own 4% fix is an easy one. It requires no discipline, organization, motivation, or caffeine: simply turn the page.

You've got this.

PART ONE: OWN YOUR TIME (OR IT WILL OWN YOU)

Almost everything will work again if you unplug it for a few minutes, including you.
—ANNE LAMOTT

YOU NEED A (GOOD) REASON TO GET OUT OF BED

I believe every human has a finite number of heartbeats.
I don't intend to waste any of mine.
—NEIL ARMSTRONG

n 2014 Helen Costa-Giles, a Canadian who now lives in Texas, was a 35-year-old mom of two who, at five feet tall and 200 pounds, was considered morbidly obese. After a doctor's visit, where she learned her weight was setting her up for a lifetime of chronic health problems, Helen knew she had to make a change. She started a workout regimen with her husband, but after her first burpee (an effective though torturous exercise that is part push-up, part squat, part plank, part *hell*, all wrapped into one movement)— when she couldn't get off the ground—she decided to never exercise again.

However, she remained committed to her health, so she put the exercise on hold to focus on nutrition. After six months, she had lost close to 90 pounds and started HIIT (high-intensity interval training) workouts—*at 4 a.m.*, because that was the only time she could fit exercise into her busy day. A chronic "everyone else gets their oxygen masks first" sort, Helen realized it was time for her to start making her health and fitness a priority.

She spent that first 4% of every day working out in her garage, the sky pitch black and the neighbourhood quiet. But while she was seeing results, she was also lonely. So she went onto her homeowners association page on Facebook and wrote, "I'm going to work out at 4 a.m. if anyone wants to join me." The following morning a neighbour showed up, and they took pictures to post to the Facebook page. The next day another neighbour came to Helen's garage at 4 a.m. Helen kept posting pictures, and people kept showing up.

"They wanted accountability as much as I did," Helen said. "But they also wanted community." And with that the No More Excuses Rise N Grind workout group was formed.

After a year—with 15 to 20 people dedicating early mornings to boot camp workouts—things got too big and loud for Helen's garage, so they moved the workouts to a local school. People were driving up to 40 minutes before the sun rose for these sessions, and soon enough other workout groups began popping up in garages in nearby neighbourhoods. What had started as one woman searching for a way to stay committed to a fitness routine had morphed into a *movement* that spread far beyond Helen's garage.

For Helen, who now runs the lifestyle coaching business

NME Lifestyle—and whose story has been featured on People.com and CNN—life has completely changed. "Six years ago, I would have been that person who said, 'I'll never be a 5 a.m. person. I'll never lose 90 pounds. I'll never be on CNN.'" Though now she takes rest days from exercise as needed, she's always up early, using that first 4% of her day for journaling, reading, even resting in the hammock and daydreaming about future goals. Helen's driving point, and one she models daily, is that we need to show up for ourselves . . . even if it means getting up at an hour we previously viewed as "off limits." And as a postscript to this story, it should be noted that every workout Helen has programmed for the past four years has contained burpees.

Like Helen, I saw one of my early-morning endeavours morph into a career, but I didn't grow up wanting to be a writer. Although I was always a voracious reader, a career in writing never occurred to me. Sure, hints of my future can be found throughout memories of my younger years: I wrote picture books of ice-skating elephants in love, and a particularly tense story of two BFF mice who had a falling out (don't worry, it had a happy ending). But even when I went back to school for journalism after five years in the corporate world, I never envisioned becoming a writer. I planned on a career in broadcasting—to become the "Katie Couric of the North"—and whenever anyone asked about my lofty writing goals, I would huff, irritably, and say, "[For the last time] I don't want to be a writer."

Then came April 10, 2003. You know when someone has a life-altering experience and she refers to the two parts of her life as "Before" and "After"? That's precisely what happened to me.

On April 9, 2003, I was a healthy, 30-year-old woman—a vegetarian who worked out most days of the week—who was finishing up her journalism school. On April 11, 2003, I got a bone marrow biopsy and had my first CT scan, because the routine follow-up appointment I'd gone to the day before had been anything but. I had non-Hodgkin's lymphoma. *Cancer.*

I was lucky for three reasons: one, I was young, so my body would likely handle treatments better; two, I was diagnosed super-early—another reason to feel hopeful; and three, as a Canadian, I had access to world-class health care. Within the year, I was finished treatment, in remission, and trying to figure out what came next. Turns out, being diagnosed with a life-threatening illness is terrifying but also, perhaps expectedly, life-affirming. Priorities go through a high-level re-org and nothing looks quite the same afterwards. But most relevant to our discussion here, it wasn't *all* bad news: I realized being an anchor, or trying to become one, was not the life I wanted after all, because it would pull me away from the things and the people I cared about most. So, *plot twist*, I became a writer.

Initially I wrote marketing and communications copy. Then, as I flexed my writer muscles and daydreamed about what came next, I started pitching magazines. I pushed myself more, deciding with stunning naïveté that it might be time to write a novel. With a journalism degree and a handful of bylines, I figured storytelling was storytelling: short form, long form, novel length. How different could it be? News flash: *very.*

Undeterred by what I didn't yet know, I immersed myself in novel writing. And as the number of pages grew, so did the significance of the project. Cancer had taken much away from me, but in return it offered two critical things:

1. I had to take my goals (a.k.a. myself) seriously, or I would never get serious about accomplishing them.

2. I wanted to leave behind a legacy for my daughter, and the idea of a published novel she could reach for—tangible and in my "voice"—seemed perfect.

Of course, *dreaming* of the thing and *doing* the thing are quite different beasts. But I'm one of those "finish what you start" types, so I stuttered and stumbled along over the next couple of years. Eventually, I wrote "The End" on that novel and . . . it sucked. Big time. But it was done, it was mine, and I could (and would) do better next time. And just like that, my "I don't want to be a writer" mantra morphed into "I *am* a writer."

I'm now the bestselling author of five novels and have a stack of magazines with stories that carry my byline, one of which won a National Magazine Award. What began as a "let's see what happens" project has blossomed into a fulfilling career that is robust and fun and, thankfully, still feels limitless—oh, and mostly happens before the rest of you get out of bed for the day. But this didn't transpire only because I set an alarm and diligently rose at 5 a.m. It's because of *what I chose to do* once I got out of bed.

There's a concept called *ikigai* (pronounced "eye-ka-guy")—it's a Japanese term that essentially means "find your reason." The concept originated in Okinawa, a Japanese island that is said to have the world's largest population of centenarians. Ikigai is about balancing passion, joy, and purpose . . . and the understanding that everything we do is connected. And specific to our conversation here, it's the belief that you need a good reason to get out of bed (outside of paying bills or tending children). Basically, if you're going to rise early, have something waiting on the other side of the alarm that is exciting and motivating. Whatever it is *must* be more enticing than snuggling deeper under the covers.

In the beginning, Helen's ikigai was a complete health transformation so she could be around long-term for her family. Mine was finishing my novel, for the personal reasons listed above. Once I achieved that first goal, my ikigai shifted from "writing a book" to "writing a book that doesn't suck."

Think about what makes you tick and what your own ikigai might be. It's okay not to have an obvious and actionable answer at the moment. The point here is not perfection but rather to engage in a simple thought exercise. So, let me ask you, "What's worth getting out of bed for?"

THE FIRST 4%

Eat a live frog first thing in the morning, and nothing worse will happen to you the rest of the day.
—MARK TWAIN

One morning in July 1981 my parents woke us up at 3 a.m. and told us to get in the rowboat. We were at our cottage, a rustic cabin my parents had built on a serene and secluded lake. My sister and I tried desperately to keep our eyes open as our parents rowed us into the middle of the lake to watch the lunar eclipse. I distinctly remember feeling groggy and annoyed—the way only a nine-year-old can—about my parents' insistence this was a "not to be missed" experience. The lake, deep and black, was smooth as glass. The only sound around us came from the rowboat's oars, squeaking as they dipped in and out of the water. Soon my dad stopped rowing and put the anchor down, and I remember seeing the glow of the eclipse, the way it was reflected back in the lake's surface.

"That's cool," I said, yawning wide. At that point I was ready to go back to bed—until I heard the first splash. Suddenly, fish were jumping all around us. A couple even landed in the boat, right at our feet. For two kids who spent hours dangling hand-caught bait from fishing rods, waiting for the fish to nibble, this felt miraculous. It was also somewhat alarming, just *how many* fish were jumping in and around the boat, but it was one of the most memorable experiences I've ever had. Something that wouldn't have happened if my parents hadn't dragged us out of bed in the middle of the night. Because by 8 a.m., a more regular wake-up time, everything was ordinary again. The eclipse was over, the fish back to hanging out well below the surface and impervious to our squirming worms, and the magical moments of that middle-of-the-night expedition a memory.

About 27 years passed between that rowboat eclipse and when I started waking up early to harness the morning's solitude for my first writing project. But in some ways my current 5 a.m. writing time is no less magical than watching those fish jump into our boat. I'm continually amazed by how much I can accomplish on a project that is meaningful to me before the rest of my house (and to a larger extent, my world) wakes up.

Before I started writing at the crack of dawn, that first 4% of my day was occupied by chaotic minutia. Think sipping coffee while blow-drying my hair, and dressing while simultaneously catching up on email. Or flying out the door with a minute to spare, a commute-ready toasted bagel in hand. My days are no less chaotic—in fact, the addition of a kid into the mix makes *everything* more chaotic—but now the first hour of my day is decidedly calmer. It might be early, but it's sublime . . . and it's all mine.

I understand that you might not be ready to come join me at 5 a.m. . . . yet. You might agree that this hour is a time of day to be cherished, but only because you get to spend it in bed. Sleep is necessary; no arguments there. However. *However* . . .

Consider what you might be missing out on. What opportunities live on the other side of your alarm clock? What experiences could you rack up—big and small—with the decision to give yourself a previously untapped chunk of time each and every day?

I would not have five novels published—including a #1 bestseller—without my 5 a.m. writing habit. It's that black and white. I realize, however, this may not be the case for everyone or for every endeavour. I have failed book projects in the mix, including ones that remain incomplete or are just plain terrible, even when I've diligently risen early and done everything right. Things don't always go smoothly, even after you're an "expert."

However, I'm unwilling to give up that first 4% of my day because something didn't go according to plan—I've bought the lifetime membership. Becoming a card-carrying member of this 4% Fix Club does take some rejigging, so let's focus on a trial membership for starters. Rather than committing to an early wake-up five to seven days a week, you could give one morning a try. And if that doesn't reduce you to a soggy, exhausted puddle, try the same thing again the following week . . . and so on, and so on. After all, if it doesn't work out, you can always go back to bed.

In my former corporate life, I worked for a husband-and-wife team who were wildly successful and also quite eccentric. They employed a life/spiritual coach, and one of the things this coach prescribed was "egg cleansing." Basically, as I remember it being explained, eggs—like, chicken eggs you buy at the grocery store—have the power to siphon out a person's negative energy. After it does its job, this "negativity egg"—which only a short time before was a regular chicken egg ready to be turned into egg salad or an omelette—is buried somewhere, ideally far away, where it won't be disturbed. It also should never be cracked en route, as the negativity will then leech into whoever is closest.

Now, although I was raised by hippie parents and try to be open-minded, I struggled with the egg thing. Then, one day my boss, the husband—well aware of my skepticism—said, with a smile, "You know, Karma, the egg works even if you don't believe it will."

It works even if you don't believe it will. It felt like a mystery wrapped in a riddle, and at the time it did little to convince me. Though if I'm being honest, I didn't want one of those eggs to crack near me, so perhaps I held a minuscule amount of belief. Regardless, his proclamation has stuck with me for two decades and counting, and I think of it often.

In the beginning, getting up earlier than you're used to will be hard; in particular because you have no proof it will work—that investing 4% of your day, at that time of day, can be a positive experience. This comes down to believing in something not yet tangible. But the reason it works—even if you're certain this early hour will consist mostly of staring soft-focused and slack-faced into space—is because *you are out of bed*. Our brains and bodies know what to do once we're awake. These intricate systems have, after all, been running all night and don't suddenly turn off once that alarm blares. And so, if you're willing to give it a try, the proof you need won't be far behind.

Ultimately, this book and I are advocating that the way to uncover more time is to, well, protect some of the time you already have. Unfortunately, there is no way to expand the hours in a day—we all have the same non-negotiable 24 hours. Imagine you have a delicious cake (my vote is for chocolate) in front of you, sliced into 24 identical segments. Each sliver of cake represents one hour of your day, and I bet you have enough cake-loving people in your life that it isn't long before half the cake is gone. Then you have to serve cake to things like commutes, exercise, errands, responsibilities, and commitments . . . Not many slices of cake left, right? But now apply the 4% fix approach and consider the whole cake again, before any slices go anywhere. Slide out one perfect sliver of cake for you to enjoy, *first and guilt-free*.

This is why my 5 a.m. writing habit works and has been sustainable over many books and many years. I choose to serve myself a slice first, so even if I spend the rest of the day doling out cake until only crumbs remain, I was able to have my cake . . . and eat it too.

SET. YOUR. ALARM.

The most difficult thing is the decision to act,
the rest is merely tenacity.
—AMELIA EARHART

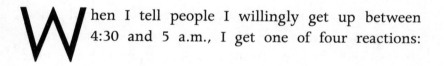hen I tell people I willingly get up between
4:30 and 5 a.m., I get one of four reactions:

1. "Why?" Translation: Nope. I already stopped listening.

2. "Wow, that's early!" Interpretation: I should take a step back in case this early-riser thing is contagious.

3. "I wish I could do that, but for reasons A–Z I simply cannot." Understood as: I don't really wish I could do that.

4. "Teach me how." Or, "What's your secret?"

This last group is the one I feel for the most, because now they've engaged me in a way they might later regret. It's fair to say I'm enthusiastic about my early-morning routine. For these folks I smile and gently say, "The secret? You already know it: Set. Your. Alarm."

The bare-bones truth about how I consistently do this is that I set an alarm every night. Even though I wake most days before said alarm, I know I have a backup. It's like the well-known slogan applied to Crockpot cooking: "Set it and forget it!"

Levi Hutchins of New Hampshire made the first mechanical alarm clock in 1787, as a way to wake himself up for work. The alarm clock was then patented in 1876, and we've been setting (and dreading) our tinny, brain-piercing wake-up machines ever since. Whether you employ an old-school clock-radio version, or your phone's alarm, or one of those clocks that rolls away from the bed, giving you no choice but to get up, the majority of us need a jumpstart to get out of bed.

As for *how* to make your alarm work for you—because snooze is a tempting option—the first thing you have to do is figure out what you want once you get out of bed.

Now comes the second part of "How the *bleep* do I do this?" You could go cold turkey and set a 5 a.m. alarm for tomorrow morning, but without preparation and organization it will be unpleasant. But if that's how you want to tackle this, okay, fine—some of us have greater pain thresholds than others. However, if you stick with me here, I can probably smooth things out for you so 5 a.m. doesn't feel like a million paper cuts dipped into lemon juice.

Now, writing is my job, and so you might be saying, "Hey, Karma, remember ground rule #3? You told us that the first 4% isn't about catching up or productivity," and you're right. So let me explain. When I wake early, I am not doing what I term "author busywork": no answering emails, no research missions, no Q&As. I save these logistical tasks for later in the day. My first hour of the day is simply about the writing, in its purest form—creating characters, building worlds, moulding prose, and channelling creativity, which is why it's straightforward (though not effortless) to get up early. Because while I do love my job, answering a marketing questionnaire will never inspire a happy 5 a.m. wake-up, know what I mean?

Time to acknowledge *you do not need to do this*. It's okay to never become a morning person. You are a grown-up and, as such, have earned the right to more or less direct your way through this world. And that includes what you wear, what you eat, when you go to bed, and how early you set your alarm clock. Some of you may already be getting up before the sun, whether for a job, for a workout, or because you're already a fan of that early hour. Others might wish to become morning larks, if only they didn't love their mattresses quite so much. And still others think this is a horrible idea and only horrible things will happen as a result. Changing anything isn't easy. But I assure you it is possible—even if it doesn't feel like it right now—to become an early riser.

There's been much talk about the connection between early rising and success: Apple CEO Tim Cook allegedly rises by 3:45 a.m.; Richard Branson "wakes with the sun" at 5:45 a.m.; Oprah Winfrey gets out of bed around 6 a.m.; and Anna Wintour, *Vogue*'s editor-in-chief, is up before 6 for an hour of tennis, then gets a blowout (because *of course*) immediately afterwards, and is hard at work by 9 a.m. A quick search finds dozens of articles with titles such as "10 Highly Successful People Who Wake Up before 6 a.m.," "Benefits of Early Risers," "6 Secrets to Success Only Early Birds Know," "Are Early Risers More Productive?" The early risers certainly think so.

Yet, while it might seem obvious that those of us up earlier have more time to get stuff done, most of us also do not have access to an endless source of energy. If I'm up before the sun, my brain shuts down somewhere around 5 p.m.; I'm useless by 9 p.m. and asleep about an hour or so later. While it's true you'll get *15 extra days* in a single year if you wake up one hour earlier each day—which seems like magic but is simple math—you will probably have to give up your night owl tendencies to cash in on that extra time.

Some of you might be thinking, *Hang on . . . it's not magically found time if I have to go to bed an hour earlier*, and you're correct. However, think about how you spend that last hour of your day. For some of you, it may be a well-used 4% and so you're wondering why you would give that up. But regardless of what you perceive as evening accomplishments, the difference between 5 a.m. and 11 p.m. is this:

your brain is a clean slate in the morning. You have slept. Everything that happened during the previous day has been compartmentalized and analyzed and stored in your memory. Overnight, your brain has categorized and tidied up your daily activities and experiences, and is refreshed and ready for anything you toss its way.

While your mind may be fresh and raring to go at 5 a.m., your body may feel like someone poured cement into it while you slept. It took me a couple of months to get into the early-bird groove. It has been years since I started rising early, and I still can't muster the muse without a hefty dose of caffeine.

We'll talk more about sleep later—and look at our slumber habits and patterns—but I would be remiss not to mention the issue of sleep deprivation. According to pretty much every sleep expert out there, the vast majority of us are chronically sleep-deprived and not getting the recommended seven to nine hours per night. When we don't get enough sleep, things go *badly*. All you need to do is live with a newborn for a month to understand that. And when we're sleep-deprived, shit hits the fan: our memory (short- and long-term) suffers, as does our alertness and performance on operational tasks such as driving a car. Even our health becomes compromised, with a menu of negative effects like raised blood pressure, mood changes, and decreased immunity. As Dr. David Dinges, a professor and sleep researcher at the University of Pennsylvania School of Medicine, says, "Everything we know about sleep loss is harmful."

The 4% fix is not about *cutting back* on sleep so you can get up earlier; it's about *shifting* your sleep schedule to accommodate the change. All I'm suggesting at this point is

10 minutes. Go to bed 10 minutes earlier, and set your alarm for 10 minutes earlier than you normally get up. And when that alarm goes off, *get out of bed*—even if you haven't yet figured out what to do with those extra minutes. It's okay to do nothing special with this newfound time yet. It's also just fine to catch up on a television show or read a chapter of a book or sit quietly and curse this "stupid idea." But the point is, you got up and owned that first sliver of your day . . . which means you now have the proof you can do it.

THE OXYGEN MASK

*When you say "Yes" to others, make sure you
are not saying "No" to yourself.*
—PAULO COELHO

I used to squeeze in writing time whenever and wherever
I could. While my daughter was at her swimming lesson,
on the rare occasion she'd fall asleep in the car on our way
home from the grocery store, when she was busy making ice
cream sundaes and caterpillars out of playdough. My strategy
was simple: as long as she was safe and relatively contained,
I could clean up any mess she created *after* my writing session. I wasn't being "selfish," focused more on the words on
the page than on what my toddler was up to; I was being
"smart," sorting out how to multi-task. And then came the
Vaseline incident.

When parents say the moment it's quiet—too quiet—is when you need to stop whatever it is you're doing and go investigate, it's because they've all had their own Vaseline incident. On this particular day, I was writing at the kitchen table, surrounded by playdough creations and leftover glitter. I was in the "zone": a state of writerly flow, the rare and magical place authors covet but can't force, a wave you must ride out while it lasts because who knows when it will come again. Then, from somewhere in the depths of my focus, a tiny alarm bell went off in my head. My fingers stalled on the keys and I paused to listen for a moment. Silence. Complete silence. *Shit.* This is bad news when you have a toddler underfoot. Silence means you will soon have deep, deep regrets.

"Where is she?" I said out loud, even though I was alone in the kitchen. "Where are you?" A small thump from upstairs and I was racing, two stairs at a time. I found my three-year-old in the washroom—completely fine— delighted with herself. "I fixed him!" she said, pointing to our labradoodle, Quincy, who was sitting beside her on the bathroom floor. He did not look fixed. He looked miserable and . . . greasy? Quincy had epilepsy and was on a new medication, and my toddler had decided, to make him feel better, she would rub him down with petroleum jelly, which was our cure-all for when her diaper rash had flared. She had covered poor Quincy head to tail with a Costco-sized jar of Vaseline, and he looked like a rat who had drowned in a vat of oil. It took multiple baths and many weeks for the Vaseline to completely wear out of his fur, and I learned the consequences of trying to wear my "mother" and "writer" hats simultaneously. It was not a good look.

If you've ever been on an airplane, you've heard the "always put on your own oxygen mask first" in-case-of-emergency instructions. This has been appropriated countless times, from self-care during job hunting to staying sane while parenting a spirited toddler to how the best leaders steer companies with the "your mask on first" lingo. Generally speaking, it's a message that resonates so broadly and across every demographic because of this simple truth: if we are always taking care of everyone else's needs before our own, we can easily become shrivelled-up, exhausted, useless, boring, stressed-out versions of ourselves. But if we don't have a solid plan in place for how to get that oxygen mask on, we might find ourselves bathing our petroleum-jelly-soaked labradoodle for days on end.

Back when I was a night owl, I only half-listened to the oxygen mask instructions on flights, which I took many of during my corporate days. *Yes, yes,* I would think, keeping most of my attention focused on my book, my laptop, my music. *I get it. Be selfish with the oxygen mask.* It seemed obvious, and was particularly simple to follow, as I was travelling alone the majority of the time. My world view carried a lot more of the "me first" mentality back then.

In the years since, I've discovered the best way to get my oxygen mask on is to protect that first hour of my day. While later in the evening might at times be more pleasant or convenient, mornings continue to be when I'm at my creative best . . . and when there are the fewest distractions in my house. So I've learned to adapt, and as my daughter's kindergarten teacher used to tell her class, "You get what you get, and you don't get upset."

Putting on your own virtual oxygen mask sounds straightforward enough, but for most of us it requires strategy, planning, and commitment. Unlike on the airplane, where it drops in front of your face during an emergency, its presence isn't as blatant in day-to-day life. Especially when we consider how our lives expand to include significant others and children. The trick to getting your mask to fit well, without leaks, is figuring out two things: how to do it and how to *sustain* it, so you can take care of everyone's needs—including your own.

My husband, a stand-up comedy fan, insisted I watch Ali Wong's *Hard Knock Wife* special. Fair warning for those inclined to queue it up: Ali Wong is funny, but her language is about as explicit as you could imagine. Which means this is not appropriate television viewing for children, nor for those who believe "Dang it!" is edgy. Most of Wong's show is about motherhood, being a wife and a woman in this day and age, and during her bit she addresses the "oxygen mask first" message. She shared that when she was travelling with her young daughter, the flight attendant explained she should always put her own mask on first, before her child's. She said she rolled her eyes and was like, "Yeah . . . I was going to do that anyway." Way to go, Ali Wong. We should all take a page out of her book.

If you're in a place in your life where nightmares involving a flight, a dozen oxygen masks, and the paralyzing anxiety of who to save first are the norm, let me put it this way: *if you don't do this, you are the cog in the wheel.* You are depriving yourself of vital oxygen—not in the literal sense, but in every other way you can imagine: emotionally, psychologically, creatively, even physically, because the mind-body connection is relevant here.

It may feel selfish to consider doing this (so many other things, and people, likely need your attention), and that's exactly the point. Think back to a time when you did something that was only for you . . . not for an employer, or a member of your family, or because of an obligation. *For you.* Then think about a pursuit you've always wanted to tackle, like learning a new language, or volunteering for a cause you care about, or joining a masters swim team, or getting your fingers back on those piano keys you haven't touched in years.

Now, maybe you can answer that you did something purely for you as recently as yesterday—*high five!*—or maybe you can't even remember the last time. Either way, here's the deal: no one else is making sure you're doing what you need to be doing or getting what you want out of this one finite life. So that leaves you in charge. But it also leaves most of us with a dilemma. Namely, in a 24-7 world driven by instant access and constant notifications, and with our jam-packed schedules, where exactly do we *find* the time?

THE FOCUSED FOUR

Your reality is created by what you focus on and how you choose to interpret it.
—Jen Sincero

I was probably about 45 years old when I (finally) realized I couldn't do it all. I spent a solid decade after becoming a mother trying to find a decent balance—and by decent, I mean I tried to figure out how to fit 36 hours' worth of stuff into a 24-hour day. I leaned in and leaned out and reprioritized and slept less and downloaded apps that forced my focus and read books and articles and asked around and bought day planners and all the while imagined it was possible. Yet despite my valiant efforts to uncover the secret, it turns out a 24-hour day is as good as you're going to get. Who knew, right? (Everyone. *Everyone knows.* But that doesn't stop many of us from trying to make it work regardless.)

In my case, the final step of learning came from a nasty knee injury. I tore my anterior cruciate ligament (ACL) while skiing and went from doing everything to sitting on my butt on the couch, trying to get around on crutches, and basically feeling quite sorry for myself. I remember one night very clearly. It was the second day after my injury, my knee looked like it was smuggling a water balloon under the skin, and I was wobbling on my crutches, trying to make dinner. After I spilled a full pot of water and nearly ended up on my ass when one crutch slipped in said spilled water, I decided enough was enough. I went back to the couch and sat my sorry ass back down, and my husband came home and made boxed macaroni and cheese, and everyone survived just fine.

Since then I've re-evaluated my time, my days, how I'm committing to my goals, and what my priorities are. And because I'm the Type A sort who finds serenity in compartmentalized priorities, I figured that if I did at least four things each day—one for my health, one for my creativity, one for my family, and one for my productivity—my own personal world would keep spinning along.

Here's how I generate my critical to-dos, on a typical day, into a *Focused Four* list. These are the mandatory items, the things that sit above work deadlines and dentist appointments and the like. And because I don't want to set up unrealistic expectations, please note that I do not write out these four items every single day—I would like to, and it's a work in progress. But even if I don't get them written down, I keep these areas of focus top of mind throughout my day. Your categories may look different from mine (maybe you'd prefer

Spiritual to Family, or Learning to Creativity, for example), and that's just fine—tweak away.

When I am on the ball and get my items down on paper, here's how my Focused Four list might read:

❑ **Health/Wellness:** One-hour workout

❑ **Creativity:** One-hour writing session starting at 5 a.m. (also my 4% fix)

❑ **Family:** Homemade dinner, eat together

❑ **Productivity:** Clean out inbox, respond to messages, and get to zero unread

Each of these takes about 1 hour (or about 4% of my day), so in my 17 or so wakeful hours, in only 4 hours I'm actually ticking off some things that not only have a significant impact on my day, but are also in line with my daily (and beyond) priorities. It's amazing that when I consider each day from this perspective, I'm able to fit things in that otherwise might fall behind.

I understand, for some, lists are not sexy; they take away the tiny bit of spontaneity you might be able to harness from the daily grind. And as such, they can be confining and annoying, and when you're already tapped out with your schedule, do you really need another reminder of just how many boxes you have yet to tick off? But lists, especially those such as the Focused Four, are crucial in keeping you honest. Not to your general to-dos, but honest to your priorities—and I'm not just talking about the daily ones here. I mean those priorities that, when your last hour on this planet is up, allow you to look back and feel positive about where you put your energy and focus. Those priorities are different for each of us, but you should absolutely have them written down somewhere. That's non-negotiable.

I have other lists I make—for groceries, appointments, bills to pay, daily chores and errands, meal preparation—but this Focused Four list is a different beast. It is less a "to-do" and more a "living my best life" sort of thing. And like so many things, once you do it for a while it becomes a habit. And habits are hard to break, which is a great thing when it comes to trying to achieve a goal or two you never imagined you could, or would, have the time for.

My suggestion is to make the list the night before. You could, in theory, do it for an entire week at a time (or longer), but in my experience, it's best to have a touch of urgency and newness for the four categories on any given day. Plus, things can shift through your week, and if you overprepare by writing down Health/Wellness, Creativity, Family, and Productivity (or whatever your own categories are) for multiple days, you could end up struggling to stay on task each day because of changes to your schedule or other unexpected things that arise.

Last thing: make this list on paper instead of digitally. I know most of our lives exist in a digital world these days, and it may seem easier to add these categories into your daily calendar and share them across your devices. There is power in the writing down of the items and taking notes by hand. But you don't have to take my word and experience for it—science backs me up.

A 2014 study of college students done by Princeton

psychological scientist Pam Mueller and psychological researcher Daniel Oppenheimer found that you'll remember information—particularly conceptual information—better over the long term if you take your notes by hand rather than on a laptop. One thing the researchers noticed is that students taking notes on laptops were more likely to capture the information verbatim, whereas note-takers, due to a lesser ability to pen quickly, had to chunk the content and record only highlights, versus a word-for-word account.

Essentially, because students could type quickly, they could transcribe the lecture exactly as they heard it. The by-hand note-takers were forced to process what they were hearing first, so they could capture the salient information for recall. The processing of the information is what made it stick, particularly when it was conceptual rather than factual.

Now, we are not talking about scores of notes here, with these mini-goal lists. However, we do want to connect as deeply as possible with what we're writing down, and by putting pen to paper, we're allowing our processing to take over. This will help get us to the strategizing and problem-solving portion of working our way through our lists.

Now is the time to come up with four categories that matter to you, and that you'd like to tackle every single day if you could swing it. If you're feeling particularly ambitious, you can capture these categories on a piece of paper (there's also a handy-dandy page for this at the back of the book). Next, consider what activities might fit under these four categories. They do not need to be time-consuming things. I generally aim for about an hour per category, but sometimes the items take much less time. For example, occasionally I meditate for my Health/Wellness activity. But because I'm new to meditation and find five minutes of mindfulness harder than almost anything else, this typically represents a 5- to 10-minute exercise. That's it. Or a Family activity could be organizing a play date for my daughter, which takes a text or two and no more than 10 minutes. Or maybe I have one critical email to compose and send, which takes less than 20 minutes but helps me tick my Productivity box for the day.

The point is not to find things that fill up your day or, alternatively, take only 30 seconds. It's important to recognize that a task taking longer does not make it a more earnest goal or activity—that's not how you should be thinking about your Focused Four lists.

Finally, not every item will be enjoyable. This is an unrealistic expectation and one sure to make you feel like you're failing. I have a dear author friend who spent most of her summer days driving her two children to a variety of camps and activities, which they often complained about profusely. She could, as a result, have checked off her Family box with "Drive ungrateful children to activities they whine about." It may not have been something that brought her—or her children, it would seem—great joy or satisfaction, but it counts, nonetheless. And because her kids were in activities (which they did, in fact, enjoy once they got there), she ended up with an hour here and there to herself, in a coffee shop between chauffeuring duties, when she could work without interruption, checking off both her Productivity and Creativity boxes.

The purpose of my Focused Four approach is to remind myself, every day, what my priorities are. I try not to be too strict with my list, or too earnest or ambitious about the items on it; otherwise, I'll end up wrestling with an untameable to-do list. Which is a depressing challenge, and more than that, an epic time-waster. And wasting time is precisely what we're trying to avoid, unless under Health/Wellness you write: *Waste an hour of time, and enjoy every minute of it!*

NEWBIE NATION

A person who never made a mistake never tried anything new.
—ALBERT EINSTEIN

I n 1965 Gail Vance Civille—a sensory scientist and founder of Sensory Spectrum, based in New Jersey—was working her first job in the field. With a degree in chemistry, she was hired as an associate sensory project leader at General Foods, where, after a few months and with no formal training, she was asked to attend a product tasting panel.

In the testing room that day were three samples of red Jell-O in front of each tester, in what Civille described as "beautiful" ceramic bowls. It was her first time on a tasting panel, and she followed the instructions precisely: *Try each sample and write down what you tasted.* So Civille did, writing *Red Jell-O, sweet* after tasting the first sample. The second sample tasted much the same, and again she noted the flavour as *Red Jell-O, sweet*. After trying the last sample, which according to Civille tasted identical to the other two, she labelled it once again with, you guessed it, *Red Jell-O, sweet*. But when she put her pencil down and looked up, she found all the other tasters (who were far more experienced than she was) still taking notes.

"I thought it was a hazing, because that's all I wrote down [*Red Jell-O, sweet*]," Civille says. "But my colleagues were writing a lot."

When it came time to divulge what those colleagues had been scribbling about, Civille discovered the issue was with the second sample. Everyone else on the panel described sample two as containing elements of "wet dog," "wet wool," or "wet sweater"—things Civille says she never tasted in any of the three samples.

Over the 50-plus years that Civille has been a professional sensory evaluator, she has not only come a long way from her *Red Jell-O, sweet* days, but has fine-tuned her skills and made significant contributions to her industry. Civille maintains that to do the sort of work she does well, having the right "equipment" is important—"You have to make sure the noses are screwed on right," she explains—but perhaps most critically, *you have to be willing to put in the work*.

When we watch people who are outstanding at something—like athletes and business leaders and musicians and artists—it can be hard to fathom that, at some point in their lives, this something they're now revered for was unfamiliar and foreign. Every one of them started with a *first moment*, and while for some it might have been before they could remember (like Lindsey Vonn, the highly decorated Olympic and World Cup ski racer, who was on skis by the age of two), others came to their outstanding *something* later in life.

Take Vera Wang, the famed wedding dress designer. Wang was actually on a completely different path, as a figure skater who unfortunately (or fortunately, if you're a fan of her designs) didn't make the U.S. Olympic team. Then, post–skating career and immediately after graduating college, Wang was hired as an editor at *Vogue* magazine. However, she was passed over for the editor-in-chief position, and so decided to start doing her own thing, which was designing wedding gowns—at the age of 40. In 2018 *Forbes* magazine placed her 34th on the list of America's Richest Self-Made Women, with revenues upwards of $630 million in that year.

Vera Wang's story is one of those that is much discussed because it's extraordinary, but it also highlights the mantra that there's a first moment for everyone and for everything. There was a time when Vera Wang's name was not synonymous with weddings and celebrities and fandom. And unlike Vera Wang, most of us are never going to reach that level of recognition. The takeaway is not that you should do a 180-degree turn and start something new with the hopes of it bringing you great notoriety and wealth (though if that happens, *amazing*), but that you should never be afraid to be at the very beginning of something. To be naive and inexperienced and uncertain about what you're doing can be awkward, frustrating, and uncomfortable, but there's also much fun in that stage if you're willing to see it that way.

One of the added benefits of starting something new? It forces you to take a look at how you're currently spending your time, and to adjust as needed, so you can carve out the space required. You will need to find and protect a block of time; otherwise, you're setting yourself up to fail before you even start. As I've already said, it isn't exactly easy to make this work, but it is simple. Your own first moment is waiting for you—all you have to do is decide you're ready to grab it.

"SELFISH" IS NOT A BAD WORD

*As you grow older, you will discover that you have two hands,
one for helping yourself, the other for helping others.*
—SAM LEVENSON

Lucas Murnaghan has worn many hats: a pediatric
orthopedic surgeon, a talented underwater photog-
rapher and artist, co-owner of a Toronto-based surf
shop, an accomplished Ironman triathlete. To say he has a
lot to squeeze into, and out of, each day is putting it mildly.
When he was training for his triathlons—which involved a
gruelling schedule of swimming, running, and cycling—in
order to keep things in balance with his work and relationships, he knew he had to figure out how to unlock more
time in his already jam-packed schedule. A fellow triathlete
shared his own strategy, which was implementing "ghost

workouts." The idea of a ghost workout is to fit training into an unnoticeable part of the day (think: late at night or very, very early in the morning) as a strategy to avoid negatively impacting the other responsibilities, and people, in your life.

Murnaghan says, "It was a way to fill negative space and to minimize the impact on my life, work, and family." For him, the optimal time to do a ghost workout was first thing in the morning—like 4 a.m. first thing—and in order to not be running on fumes, he altered his schedule to go to bed earlier. Admittedly, he says, he has always been a morning person, so the transition wasn't earth-shattering for him. Working out late at night, as an alternative, didn't jibe with Murnaghan's schedule because the workouts delayed his ability to fall asleep, which was bad news for his early-morning surgeries.

Overall, Murnaghan felt he could get more done in that first hour of the day than in a block of time (say, three hours) later on, mostly because of the no-distractions thing. It has been such a successful schedule shift for him that, along with his Ironman training, Murnaghan has also applied this principle to his creative and academic work.

Anyone who has trained for some type of race or has taken on a personal goal with a significant commitment knows that it can seem selfish to invest the time required, as it inevitably takes time away from something, or some-one, else. When my husband and I were training for a half-marathon, we traded off run schedules: I would get in my required mileage once he was home from work (I was on maternity leave at the time), and he would either go after me or go first thing in the morning. On the weekends we literally high-fived as he came in from his run and I set out.

And it worked—we were both ready for the race, and our daughter always had one of her parents with her—but I will admit to missing time with my husband during that three-month period. Because the hours we might normally have spent together chilling out were instead spent running solo. At times it felt selfish to go for a two-hour run, especially when it meant siphoning from our family time. But with only a finite number of hours in a day, if you want to accomplish a goal outside of your regularly scheduled activities, something else has to give.

"Selfish" is a loaded word, used liberally across ages and stages. We tell our kids not to be selfish and to share their toys when their friends come over to play; we apply the term to young people focused on work and little else; and we toss it around in our relationships. We have the tendency to negatively judge anyone taking time away from something— or someone—as being "selfish." Millennials often bear the brunt of this, as they more than any other generation seem to strive to find a realistic balance between work and the rest of their lives, which typically requires non-negotiable "self-care" time.

But perhaps we're looking at this idea of selfishness all wrong. Our society certainly rewards *selflessness* and expects it of many (especially parents). However, as with the oxygen mask analogy, if we're always giving to others without considering our own needs, we will have nothing left to keep ourselves going. You need to find a way to prime the pump so the fuel (energy) required is available and in place. Barbara Kingsolver, the author of *The Poisonwood Bible*, started writing at 4 a.m. because, as she said, that's "when no one needs me." She was able to carve out time to write in the quiet, pre-dawn hours before her family roused, and could then stop her workday to re-engage with her family at dinnertime. Though 4 a.m. does admittedly feel borderline "middle of the night" even to this morning lark, it was a strategy that worked well for Kingsolver. Not only is she a prolific bestselling and award-winning novelist, writer, poet, essayist, and science journalist, but she also simultaneously raised two children.

Like Murnaghan and Kingsolver, you may have to be creative about where you find the time to do your thing that doesn't fit within the confines of your regular daily schedule. And while hopping on your bike at 3 a.m. may sound bananas and fall into the category of "absolutely never," consider where you might be able to find a block of time within your day. For me and for those with whom I've shared my 5 a.m. creative writing habit, that first 4% of the day is the ideal time to uncover a secret hour or two. As we've already discussed, you tend not to have as many distractions at 5 a.m. as you might later on in the day. Being awake while everyone else is still asleep affords you the luxury of peace and quiet, which is a hot commodity for most of us these days.

GO TO BED

A ruffled mind makes a restless pillow.
—CHARLOTTE BRONTË

I t's not about wake time, it's about bedtime.

This chapter could probably consist of only the sentence above. The key to success isn't getting up earlier, it's getting to bed earlier. However, you didn't pick up this book for one-sentence chapters, so I'll elaborate.

When you think about waking up early—let's say 5 a.m., or a time that's at least an hour before your regular rising time—what comes to mind? Probably how tired you'll feel, because you are in the camp of believing hour x to still be prime sleep time. But that's because you're only thinking of one end of things. It's true that if you maintain your current sleep schedule, particularly if you're a dedicated night owl and can't imagine falling asleep before midnight, you will feel awful when your alarm goes off.

As I'll talk about in the sleep chapters, adults need a minimum of seven to nine hours of slumber per night to perform optimally. Losing even one hour from that optimal number can have significant consequences on your ability to perform simple yet critical tasks, like driving with decent reaction times. The science isn't a slam dunk, but some studies have shown a brief increase in both car accidents and heart attacks in the days following the change to daylight savings time in the spring, when our clocks jump ahead one hour. And while most of us try to compensate for a lack of shut-eye with hacks like coffee, no amount of caffeine will change how your body and brain deal with chronic tiredness. When we're tired, our willpower suffers, as does our focus. And you need both if you're planning to start something new.

Let's turn our attention to the other end of things—bedtime. Why do you stay up late, if you do? Is it because that's the only quiet time you can find in a day, and it's when you relax with a book, television show, or some other sort of entertainment? Or is it when you connect with your significant other, because every other hour of your day is spoken for? If you really and truly can only find free time between the hours of 10 p.m. and 2 a.m., then hey, you do you. Most days we are all just doing our best.

My husband loves his sleep. Like, he would choose it— and often does—over watching a movie or reading in the evening or doing something else others would find relaxing and a good use of downtime. When we first started dating, he used to sleep heavily right up to his alarm, then snooze once or twice, and then race to get up and get ready for work. He had it practically down to a science: he could time it almost to the minute, how long he could stay in bed and still account for a shower, traffic delays, a stop for a coffee (and so on), so he arrived at work on time. But it made him miserable, even if it was an impressive time-management feat. Essentially, he felt as though he started working the second his alarm went off. With no buffer time between his alarm and the get-ready routine, he was on edge and irritable from the get-go.

These days he gets up by 5:45 a.m. so he can eat a quick breakfast and get to the gym for 6:30, after which he does the usual get-ready-for-work thing. By the time he starts his workday, he has already exercised and had a few minutes to relax, and he's in a much better space for his day. Of course, he also used to go to bed much later, which messed with his morning mojo. Now, going to bed earlier allows him to get up earlier, ensuring he doesn't feel like he's on the hamster wheel of life.

Most of us will face a real dilemma when we decide we might give this 5 a.m. or early-morning thing a try . . . that is, it's easier said than done. It is not as simple as setting your alarm one hour earlier and achieving the desired result, which is to be awake, alert, and ready to tackle whatever you set your alarm for, and then able to coast through the rest of the day without fatigue. *Not gonna happen.*

Essentially, if you wake up an hour earlier cold turkey, you have created an at-home jet-lag-like situation—and you will feel about as great (which is to say, *terrible*) as you do when flying across time zones and ending up hours behind

51

or ahead of where your body and brain think you are. And there's a good reason why: our biological clocks are set and are not easy to tweak.

Research has shown that one of the biggest culprits in making it harder to get up in the morning is our production of melatonin—the sleep hormone. Without rising melatonin cueing our bodies that it's time to go to sleep, we will remain alert. Melatonin production is set to our circadian rhythms (*circadian* is Latin for "about a day") and is heavily influenced by a variety of factors, including alcohol. So for those who are not teetotalers, this explains why we don't always sleep well after indulging in late-night libations.

One of the worst offenders for suppressing our natural melatonin production is light, specifically blue light, which is what's emitted by those screens and devices—phones, tablets, laptops—we love to take to bed with us. Blue light is also more prevalent in the eco-friendlier fluorescent and light-emitting diode (LED) bulbs, which means we're getting more blue light these days than we ever have. And this could be messing big time with your sleep cycle. However, artificial light (in particular blue light) *can* help us during the day, as it gives a boost to attention and improves reaction times.

Since melatonin is suppressed by blue light, if you use your phone, tablet, or laptop in the evening, it will take longer for your melatonin levels to rise. Which results in it taking longer for you to fall asleep. And then, because your melatonin levels rose later, the hormone will continue to be present in your body later in the morning and—*ding-ding-ding*—that's going to make it a hell of a lot harder to get out of bed earlier. You'll feel sleepier when that alarm goes off, as your body will still be dealing with melatonin, and the cues for a more natural wake-up (a rise in body temperature, a reduction of melatonin, an increase in cortisol) won't have kicked in.

The solution is to begin transitioning to an earlier bedtime so you can transition to an earlier wake time. But the increments of time you push things back should be small to start with—try 10 minutes the first evening and subsequent morning. And perhaps avoid things like coffee or tea after 2 p.m., as the caffeine will interfere with your natural melatonin levels and make it likely you won't be tired enough to fall asleep. As well, eliminate blue light from the bedroom at least 30 to 60 minutes before bed. Full stop. If we only take in natural light from the sun, our hormones rise and fall in a predictable pattern based on the light and dark of the sun rising and setting. Adding artificial light from televisions, computers, smartphones, and even LED lighting in bedside lamps, means our bodies—specifically our circadian rhythms—get screwed up and confused.

If you *must* expose yourself to blue light in the evening, you can try wearing blue-light-blocking glasses, though the jury's still out on whether they do a good enough job of preventing the less-than-ideal effects of artificial light on sleep cycles. Or you can dim your devices or use a short-wavelength-suppressing app that tells your phone, for example, not to deliver blue-light waves so close to bedtime.

Bottom line: sleep is a thorny, complex issue (which is why we aren't finished with it yet—there's more in the next section), as are the reasons why we struggle to get enough of it. So let's circle back to the one-sentence mantra from the beginning of this chapter: *It's not about wake time, it's about bedtime.* And with that, whichever solution—or combination of strategies—allows you to get to bed earlier so you can *get up* earlier, is the right one.

CREATURES OF HABIT(S)

I keep to this routine every day without variation. The repetition itself becomes the important thing; it's a form of mesmerism. I mesmerize myself to reach a deeper state of mind.
—HARUKI MURAKAMI

Brad Isaac was a young comedian just starting out when one night he ended up at a club where Jerry Seinfeld was performing. He was able to catch up with the king of comedy backstage, and asked Seinfeld if he had any tips for a newbie on the comedy circuit. The story goes that Seinfeld told Isaac the way to be a better comic was to write better jokes, and the way to write better jokes was to write every day. Every day. He told Isaac to get a wall calendar and hang it somewhere he would see it regularly, then, with a red marker, put a big *X* through each day he wrote. He explained that, after a few days, Isaac would see a chain of those *X* marks, and after a few weeks, that long chain would be pretty satisfying. Isaac's only job, Seinfeld told him, was to not break the chain.

This has been referred to as the "Seinfeld Strategy." One of the main reasons it works is because it removes the pressure of focusing on a huge accomplishment (for Isaac, to deliver the *best ever* comedic performance, à la Jerry Seinfeld) and moves your gaze instead to a smaller, more manageable and results-based goal: write every day. It's process-based rather than performance-based, so it isn't about how "on" Isaac might feel during a performance, or how motivated he is, but rather about growing the chain of *X* days. A simple, habit-focused task.

We talk a lot about habits—particularly when it comes to things like exercise—and there's a long-standing belief that you can create a new habit in 21 days. But research shows that perhaps we don't need to focus so much on the 21-day thing, because we actually create habits without even realizing we're doing it. Wendy Wood, a psychology and business professor at the University of Southern California, found that 40% to 45% of our daily behaviours are in fact habits. Have you ever had the experience of getting in your car, starting to drive, and then ending up at your destination with no real recollection of the drive there? It's because you were driving on rote, or by habit.

Along with being daily behaviours, habits can also be traced to a predictable pattern of cue and reward. For example, the smell of coffee brewing in the morning is a cue that triggers my habit to sit down and write. Once I pour that coffee and start writing (my habit), my reward is watching the words multiply on the page. It's with this reward that dopamine, the feel-good hormone, gets released in my brain. And because our brains *love* dopamine, we're motivated to jump back on the cue-and-reward train, essentially reinforcing and solidifying the habit. Coffee leads to writing, which leads to a goal achieved, which leads to dopamine release, which leads to the desire to do it all again, which leads to a habit-forming behaviour.

You don't have to look far to see this habit loop (cue + reward) in action in your own daily life. When was the last time your phone gave you a notification ping? At some point today, unless you've turned off all notifications or don't partake in social media, you probably received an alert that someone liked or commented on one of your posts. Every time your device pings at you, a shot of dopamine gets released in your brain, flooding it with feel-good sensations. And that release of dopamine ensures you'll continue your habit of picking up your phone, posting to social media, and then waiting for the next notification and dopamine-releasing ping. This is why our phones—and social media platforms—are so habit-forming, and why we have a difficult time setting our devices aside for any length of time. It's also why, when we're bored, tired, stressed, or depressed, we reach for our phones, anticipating the hit of dopamine that's the reward for the habit of picking up our device. This can obviously create less-than-desirable habits and experiences (apparently, 80% of us have felt our phone vibrate with a notification despite the phone actually being still—this phenomenon even has a name: phantom vibration syndrome) and suck up time that could be used better elsewhere.

Amy Brann, a speaker and the author of *Make Your Brain Work: How to Maximize Your Efficiency, Productivity and*

Effectiveness, describes how routine reinforces the neural connections in our brains, and how we can strengthen those connections, thereby strengthening our habits. Neutrons—uncharged particles—are drawn to electrochemical activity, and the more you can "light up" a new circuit in the brain (so, for example, a new habit of getting up at 5 a.m.), the stronger that circuit becomes. Interestingly, our brains don't distinguish between real and imagined behaviours when we're lighting up circuits, so even imagining or mentally picturing the behaviour can help strengthen a habit without you having to perform the task.

Let's say you want to get up early to start a new daily habit, maybe writing in a gratitude journal. That first morning, when you're still lying in bed after your alarm goes off, try to imagine yourself sitting in a comfy chair while you write in your journal. Brann explains that simply *imagining* the thing you want to be doing helps boost the habit of it . . . without the physical act of doing it. Which is a pretty cool and low-effort way to ease yourself into a new early-morning habit.

However, remember that even if you're strengthening those neural connections and laying the foundation for a habit with this technique—at least within the confines of your brain—those journal pages will remain blank unless you actually put pen to paper at some point.

IS IT A BHAG OR A PHAG?

If you think you are too small to be effective, you have never been in the dark with a mosquito.
—BETTY REESE

When my daughter was a newborn, my Type A, former "oxygen mask first" self was shell-shocked. Never had I been so completely frazzled or unproductive. Yes, *yes*, I was raising a human. But my ability to Get Shit Done was compromised. And by compromised, I mean it had disappeared. It was a bit of an ego flattener, because my productivity was something I took great pride in. So, to prop up my productivity, I created a list of items I could finish within two minutes:

- Wash baby bottles

- Feed the dog

- Put in a load of laundry

- Eat a muffin

- Make a pot of coffee

- Pay a bill

- Apply nipple cream

What I was really suffering from—outside of greasy hair and no idea what day of the week it was—was a failure to achieve the BHAG (pronounced "bee-hag") I had set out for myself as a new mom and writer with ambitious goals. I had things to do, words to get down on the page, articles to slay!

If you've never heard of BHAG, it's an abbreviation for "Big Hairy Audacious Goal"—a term coined by Jim Collins and Jerry Porras in their 1994 book, *Built to Last: Successful Habits of Visionary Companies*—and regularly makes an appearance in a company's vision statement or on social media posts around the "new year, new you" theme. Here are a few notable examples of BHAGs in the world:

- **Google:** Organize the world's information and make it universally accessible and useful.

- **Microsoft:** A computer on every desk and in every home.

- **Volvo:** By 2020 no one should be killed or seriously injured in a new Volvo.

My BHAG when I became a mom?

- **Karma Brown:** Raise an exceptional human AND get an article placed in every Canadian magazine.

Though I can't help but imagine a hairy monster dripping slime from its mouth (not dissimilar to the ones in the childhood classic *Where the Wild Things Are*) when I hear the term "BHAG," that isn't what disturbs me most about this acronym. It's the whole "go big or go home" idea, which can ultimately overwhelm us and lead to action paralysis—the death of every well-intentioned goal and the bane of any hopeful goal setter. Meaning, you've brainstormed such a large goal you can't even see the building blocks holding it up, and that's precisely where your focus needs to be. Otherwise, it's not unlike trying to climb a mountain made of foam blocks stacked together.

The above-mentioned corporate BHAGs are all ginormous goals, the pie-in-the-sky kind of stuff you would expect from visionary companies (and delusional, Type A, first-time mothers) with a long reach and plenty to gain from such goals. And while they could be considered motivational, or in some cases, downright revolutionary (like Volvo's goal of no one being killed in one of their new cars), setting yourself up with an unachievable BHAG is frustrating as hell.

When, between book projects, I decided to apply my first 4% (a.k.a. the 5 a.m. Writers Club) to writing a 60-minute television pilot, I had one goal in mind: *to have fun*. I have been writing professionally for over 10 years, both fiction and non-fiction, and within those categories have written everything from a how-to piece about kids in wedding ceremonies to novels exploring the tremendous burden of grief. All of my projects have been different and challenging in their own ways, and that is one of the best parts of being a writer: every day is different.

However, I had to be careful with my "for fun" screenplay project. It's tempting to romanticize the work around a project like that (screenwriting is sexy, and ultra-creative, and exciting, and money-making . . .) and slap a flashing "Big Hairy Audacious Goal Alert" sign on it. Granted, I wasn't on contract for this pilot, and therefore no one was waiting to read, critique, or help me mould it into something saleable. It was just for me—for my own curiosity and to see if I *could* do it. I called it a PHAG (a Petite Hairless Agreeable Goal)—feel free to adopt this term if you like—and by doing so, avoided the tailspin when I only managed to finish half of it. I'll go back to it eventually, or I won't. But either way, it was fun.

My first novel fell into that same PHAG category. Truly, it stemmed from curiosity and a bullheadedness about pulling it off, and similarly I had no expectations for it. At the time I *was* a writer, but mostly of marketing and communications copy. I knew nothing about writing fiction; I was merely a lifelong consumer. Much as being a rabid hockey fan does not prepare you to play in the NHL, reading voraciously didn't help me write a bestseller. I quickly realized my BHAG versus PHAG option and chose the latter. With the only criteria being to finish the novel, I was in complete control of both the goal and result.

There will be some who disagree with me, who feel setting a BHAG forces you to S T R E T C H your focus and creativity and willingness to chase something down. That even if you don't necessarily reach the goal itself, the by-products that come from the journey will be worth it. If you've used BHAGs before in this way, to force a commitment to mini-goals on the way to a larger goal, and it has worked for you, congratulations! You've cracked the code, at least for what works for you. But if you find yourself losing stamina as you chase this Big Hairy Audacious Goal up and down hills and valleys (BHAGs can be slithery things), maybe now's the time for a PHAG approach.

I propose you start small. When I wrote my first novel, I wasn't thinking about the 80,000 words I would have at the end. I was thinking about each chapter, one at a time. On a similar note, take this very book you're reading. I was working on the first draft during the summer, and because I had committed to "Mom Camp" for most of the summer, it meant my writing time was seriously squeezed. Zoo days and ice cream trips and art projects are not conducive to manuscript writing, so I worked from about 5 to 7:30 each morning, after which I was available for my daughter and our "summer of fun" bucket list.

Breaking it down further, I knew that in order to have a first draft ready by my deadline, I needed to write 500 words a day. So, about two pages of writing. Not only was it manageable (at least most days), but this mini-goal of 500 words a day resulted in the achievement of a much larger goal: a finished first draft by deadline. A small, daily commitment equalled a large return—without the time-wasting anxiety or self-doubt that can come with a BHAG-type project. *Small start, big finish*. Or, embrace the PHAG, friends.

FEAR NOT

Everything you've ever wanted is on the other side of fear.
—GEORGE ADDAIR

We have a spider living in our bathroom that has been there longer than I thought spiders lived. I suffer from mild arachnophobia, despite *insisting* that all spiders be humanely removed from the house, so letting this spider remain as though she pays rent is somewhat out of character. However, the other day, as she walked across the ceiling, I thought, *You know what, spider? You can stay. And as long as you don't crawl into my mouth while I sleep, we can co-exist.*

There's fear that is irrational, fear that keeps you safe, and fear that holds you back. And while it should be easy to sort out which type you're experiencing, that isn't always the case: sweaty palms, a racing heart, and general unease exist regardless of whether your fear is baseless, related to your safety, or keeping you from experiencing something awesome. So it's a good idea to try to take stock of your fears, and perhaps categorize them (which helps a hell of a lot in figuring out how to deal with them).

Take my arachnophobia. It's irrational and downright silly, because I have never been bitten by a spider, nor has one crawled into my mouth while I'm sleeping (as far as I know). Plus, I'm a million sizes bigger than any spider living in my bathroom. Healthy fear that keeps me safe shows up in a variety of ways: wearing my seatbelt in the car; not climbing into the lion's enclosure at the zoo for a cuddle; staying a good few feet back from the edge of cliff lookouts and subway tracks; not mixing boozy drinks with Red Bull. I also have a fear of flying, and while I know I'm safer on an airplane than in a car, I feel much safer on the road than I do in the air. This is definitely a fear that could hold me back if I chose not to fly as a result.

A lot of this comes down to control: in my experience, it's easier to deal with fear or worry when it involves something controllable. But when it stems from something I have zero control over (like flying, because I am not a pilot), I like to take a somewhat bossy and stern approach to fear. And so I demand things of the universe and my own subconscious and throw in a little visualization for good measure. For example, "Dear universe: this plane will land safely, and it will be an excellent flight with no turbulence, thank you very much! There will also be an empty middle seat beside me. Talk soon."

My expectation is that the plane will land safely (otherwise I would never fly), but of course the no-turbulence and empty-middle-seat requests may not transpire. However, if I've managed my fear at the outset of the experience, I'm much better at handling any unpleasant surprises in the moment.

Fear can be the mother of all barriers, and we often erect it as a protectionist strategy. If we don't *try,* we can't *fail.* But a fear of success can be an obstacle too. Valentina Giangregorio is an athlete, as well as a CrossFit and nutrition coach. She's in her mid-50s and works hard—every single day—on her fitness and strength. As she was training for a 2019 CrossFit qualifier event, we talked about what would come next if she made it through. Val was deeply frustrated that her weaknesses remained weaknesses, despite her training. For example, she felt her handstand walks were subpar. (But if you can even *get into* a handstand position, you're doing pretty good, am I right?) However, she also admitted that she wasn't sure what she wanted to do about the weaknesses aspect, because if she turned those weaknesses into strengths, she might have even greater success.

"Hang on," I said. "Are you afraid of succeeding?" Most often we think about people being afraid of *not succeeding*—we all know what it's like to go for something we really want and not get it. But being afraid of success is an entirely separate issue, though no less significant in terms of its implications. For Val, success would have meant a major boost in training hours, and she was concerned about what that would do to her family and life balance. I won't say she was sabotaging her ability to handstand walk the length of the gym floor, but she certainly wasn't telling herself she was confident she could do it, either.

When you think about getting up at 5 a.m. to reclaim lost time, and how you might explain what you're doing to someone who hasn't read this book . . . what do you say? Is any part of you afraid the person will laugh either at the incredulity of it (who gets up at 5 a.m. when they don't absolutely have to?) or, worse, at *why* you're doing it? There's some minor-level risk involved in dipping a toe into the 4% fixer waters. You might feel tired. You might find consistency a challenge. You might struggle to sort out what you want to do in that newfound hour. You also might fear really going for it and then not seeing results. The best news, however, is that you are in control here. Both in how you choose to spend your time and in how you manage any hint of fear you have around it.

While I have not found a consistently successful approach to obliterating a fear-led sense of insecurity, I *have* learned it will pass. Whenever you're 100% certain you cannot do the thing you have set out to do, look to past accomplishments as proof you have the capability and the chops. And then don't convince yourself otherwise.

EVERYONE OUT OF THE POOL!

You have to have confidence in your ability, and then be tough enough to follow through.
—ROSALYN CARTER

Growing up on a farm in rural Canada meant there were limits to our entertainment choices. In the nearby small town was the library, a bowling alley, and a community centre, which meant we spent a significant amount of time in the community centre's pool. And everyone who has ever swum in a community pool knows that when the lifeguard blows the whistle and yells "Everyone out of the pool!" you get out *immediately*. Because it probably means some kid has either thrown up into the water *or worse*.

This "clear the deck" mentality also translates to the intentions you set around a first 4% routine. "Everyone out of the pool!" in my house means that from 5 to 7 a.m. I am generally unavailable. The water around me (a.k.a. the bubble of space I occupy as I sit in my "writing" chair) should be seen as not safe for swimming, and anyone who disturbs this virtual water is doing so at their own risk. It works mostly because my family members know the drill, and quite frankly, have their own morning routines. My husband gets up, eats a banana, and goes to the gym before he heads to work. And my child—the one who never used to sleep—has now discovered her own morning bubble, which sees her wrapped like a burrito under the covers until about 7 a.m.

I could go to the office or another room with a closed door, but I've found I'm most creative when not confined. There may be mornings where there's more foot traffic near my bubble, or more pressure being put on my focus—some days, there are trade-offs. However, my intentions for my time are clear . . . and not only so those around me understand, but also so *I understand.*

Because surprise, surprise, you can be your own worst enemy when it comes to sabotaging best intentions. Blame the kids. The job. The significant other. The internet. But in many cases, the problem is *you.* Remember when I said if you refuse to put on your own oxygen mask first, you are the cog in your wheel?

So how do you apply this commitment to your own routines? How do you ensure your best intentions are not being sabotaged?

Everyone out of the pool!

Basically, protect your space and time and treat it with the same reverence you would the lifeguard who blows that whistle to clear the pool.

In this case, "everyone" is a stand-in for whatever is barricading your way. This could be actual people you love dearly but who don't always respect the boundaries of your focus bubble. There may also be physical limitations to your ability to focus, like a cramped space where you don't have room for the set-up you need. In our early days together, my husband and I lived in a teeny-tiny condo in downtown Toronto—600 square feet. Now, in some places, like New York City, that's positively spacious, but it was small enough that you literally could see the other person at all times from any spot in the condo.

Other things that limit us and muddy the waters: a lack of energy; sleep deprivation; analysis paralysis; the concept of perfection; procrastination; fear; imposter syndrome. Each of these barriers can be catastrophic to our ability to create and maintain that focus bubble.

So, everyone—and every thing, excuse, or barrier—out of the pool.

It may not be feasible for you to clear a space where you are guaranteed no distractions. You may share walls with neighbours, and so working on your electric guitar skills at 6 a.m. would fall under "prohibited activities." You might have to compromise if you have children who rise early—they might inadvertently become part of your 4% fix until you can figure out how to get that time back for yourself.

Try to recall the last time you completed something free of distraction. Can't quite remember? Distraction is so much a part of our fabric of daily life that it becomes something we can count on, and also something we lament when it shows up to pull us off our focus track.

However, distraction is also something we ourselves create as a mechanism to avoid doing a thing that is challenging. This tactic naturally goes hand in hand with procrastination—we are most excellent at avoidance when we don't want to do something that ranks higher on the unpleasantness scale. I am often on the hunt for a diversion when I'm doing a mundane task like folding and putting away laundry, one of my most loathed household tasks. Without question, some urgent work matter will arise when I'm elbow-deep into trying to find matching socks in a basket of laundry. Anything to distract myself from the tedious task in front of me . . . which if I would simply give it the small amount of attention it needs, would be over and done in no time.

Conversely, if I'm on a tight deadline and am stuck as to how to pull it all together, it's amazing how critical matching my socks from the laundry pile can be—anything to avoid having to focus on the more difficult task of stitching words together into something readable. I call it "distraction procrastination" (and you know things are bad when I'm procrastinating via the laundry hamper).

The antithesis to distraction is focus, but it isn't simple to flip the switch. Even if we manage to eliminate the physical interruptions around us (by closing a door or turning off phone alerts), we remain linked to perhaps the greatest diversion of all: our own distraction-seeking brains.

Let's talk more about focus for a moment. Perhaps you've already honed some fantastic ways to force focused time into your day. The best way I can help myself with this is to stay off the internet—the absolute greatest time suck in this modern world. But another recommended strategy I've found useful is to take regular breaks. This can seem counterintuitive, because isn't the whole idea here to keep yourself focused on the task at hand for as long as it takes to complete it? Well, yes and no. Yes, you need to find ways to stay focused in order to ensure the thing gets done, but you also need to know when to step away so your energy and attention can reset. A quick coffee break or walk around the block or even a short nap can do wonders for your focus.

In *Hyperfocus: How to Be More Productive in a World of Distraction*, Chris Bailey highlights research on how often we pull ourselves away from a task . . . and how long it takes us to get back to it. Believe it or not, on average, people only focus for 40 seconds and then take 26 minutes to get back to the task at hand. Which obviously has huge repercussions on work productivity and office management. However, if you plan unplugged time—let's say you focus on a task for 15 minutes at a time, then take a short break—it becomes easier to ignore distractions and avoid procrastination.

In a study involving violinists, researchers including psychologist Anders Ericsson found that the cream-of-the-crop performers practised in a similar way: three 90-minute sessions in the morning, with a break between each session. Interestingly, a similar pattern was discovered among top performers in other fields, including athletes, writers, and even chess players. Basically, the secret sauce recipe for optimal performance seems to be short bursts of work with breaks and rest in between.

Think about your own routines and what's in the way of you being able to bask in and engage with that first 4% of your day with greater focus. Hopefully, the distractions are few and surmountable. But regardless of how many people are in your bubble or how complex it might be to "clear the pool," know that you get points for even showing up. Especially if you show up at 5 a.m.

PART TWO: FIND YOUR TIME (IT MIGHT BE EARLIER THAN YOU THINK)

I remember one morning getting up at dawn. There was such a sense of possibility. You know, that feeling. And I . . . I remember thinking to myself: So this is the beginning of happiness, this is where it starts . . . It was happiness. It was the moment, right then.
—THE HOURS (SCREENPLAY, BY DAVID HARE)

THE MARSHMALLOW TEST

You must have discipline to have fun.
—JULIA CHILD

There's a famous experiment on willpower and delayed gratification called the Marshmallow Test, which was run in the 1960s by a Stanford University researcher named Walter Mischel and featured kids and, you guessed it, marshmallows. Mischel had a four-year-old daughter at the time and put her in a room with a few other four-year-old kids, who each had a solitary marshmallow set in front of them. He then told them he was going to leave the room for 10 minutes, and if they still had that marshmallow in front of them when he returned, they would get a *second* marshmallow.

Marshmallows are delicious and hard to resist even if you're ten times the age of these kids, so this was a high-stakes situation for this group of preschoolers. Any guess how many of them were able to resist eating that first marsh-mallow in those 10 minutes? As you might expect, only a small percentage (10% to 15%) still had a marshmallow in front of them when Mischel returned. He published his study, but it didn't garner much attention—it seems not a lot of people found kids eating, or not eating, marshmal-lows (and in later studies, cookies and pretzels) all that enlightening.

But then, as the story goes, a few years later, when Mischel's daughter was in grade five, he was talking to her about her day at school and she shared some tidbits about the kids in her class. And that was when things really clicked for Mischel—he realized the kids who were anec-dotally, according to his daughter, doing well in school were some of the same ones who had been able to resist the first marshmallow six years earlier.

Mischel tracked these middle school–aged kids down and then followed them through high school, on to college, and beyond. It was one of the largest longitudinal studies ever done, and amazingly Mischel discovered that the kids who had resisted the marshmallow at age four were statis-tically significantly more successful than their peers. They had better jobs, higher salaries, and longer marriages, to name a few of the positive life outcomes Mischel found. But before we go sitting our children down with a marshmallow on a paper plate and 10 minutes on the clock, it's import-ant to note that a later study tried to replicate Mischel's findings (and this one was significantly larger and more diverse), but it observed only about half the effect of the original study.

Regardless, it leads to an interesting question: Can you teach people willpower, or are we essentially split into those who would immediately eat the one marshmallow and those who think two marshmallows is better than one, and worth waiting for?

Personally, I don't believe it's quite that clear-cut, that will-power is either lacking or present. Instead, I see willpower as something that simply ebbs and flows . . . depending on the day, or maybe even the hour. We've all experienced this: you make a commitment to start doing something, or to stop doing something, and some days it's easier to stay on track than others. When I wrote an article about sugar years ago, my entire family went sugar-free for 30 days. On the "do not eat" list were artificial sweeteners, but also those people call "natural sugars"—honey, maple syrup, agave—which I had learned, thanks to an interview with a physician who researched obesity, broke down in our bodies in an identical way to basic white or brown sugar. "Your body doesn't care if it comes from a tree or a bee," this doctor told me. "Sugar is sugar."

This was tough news for my husband, in particular, who has a serious sweet tooth. Thankfully, we were already a family that ate pretty healthily, and because I was a work-at-home mom at the time, much of what we ate was home-made. But the more I read labels, the more items were scratched off the list, and things got pretty dark for a while there. Especially when I tried to replicate my banana muffins using a dried date paste (fruit, either fresh or dried unsweet-ened, was allowed) instead of sugar. They were just this side of edible.

I think our daughter had the easiest time that month. I managed, and my husband suffered sugar-withdrawal agony on a nightly basis for the first two weeks. We did eventually break down and have a glass of wine, deciding that as parents of a fiery preschooler, it was a lifesaving decision for all of us. But the reason our willpower stayed mostly intact throughout the sugar-free month wasn't because we were particularly superhuman with our staying-on-track skills. Rather, it was because I had planned the month ahead of time, stocking the pantry and fridge with sugar-free options to ensure staying on the wagon was possible when things got tough.

A month, cold turkey, is a long time to go without something as prevalent as sugar (it is added to *everything*). Even with preparation and steely commitment, there were days we almost gave in. When it comes to finding willpower day to day, preparation is key—future you can thank past you for the foresight—but it's also important to decide what motivates you best to stay on track. As a journalist, I'm a geek about education and knowledge, so I was highly motivated that month to see the experiment through and to be able to write about what I learned. But when it comes to my 5 a.m. writing goals, or any task that, while I really want to accomplish it, is challenging, I like to employ rewards for willpower.

Here's how that works: I assign myself a reward for finishing the task, just like I did for my potty-training child. Rewards can be anything—I prefer jelly beans or chocolate, or maybe the purchase of a new book I've been coveting—but you must not sneak one of those jelly beans in before the job is done, no matter how tempting; otherwise, you're rewarding yourself for *not* having willpower.

Regardless, if you're feeling as though your willpower is limping along right now, and the thought of putting even more pressure on it with an early wake-up feels impossible, not to worry. Go ahead and eat that marshmallow, and relieve yourself of the guilt for doing so. The beauty of life is that each day resets the moment you open your eyes, and you get another 24 slices of cake and a brand-new shot at stocking up marshmallows, no matter what happened the day before.

RATION THE ROADBLOCKS

Most of the shadows of this life are caused by standing in one's own sunshine.
—RALPH WALDO EMERSON

Procrastibaking. If you don't know what this is or have never engaged in this activity, here's the deal: procrastibaking is baking as a procrastination strategy. And a lot of people are doing it. A quick search for the hashtag #procrastibaking on Instagram currently brings up 41,000 posts, including a few of my own.

If you find me whipping up a batch of blueberry muffins or banana bread any weekday mid-afternoon, you can bet I'm procrastinating. Because, as the "I want to focus, please" side of me likes to argue, no one *needs* baked goods to survive. The truth is—and I've become adept at recognizing it—baking makes me feel productive (Fresh-baked banana bread! You're welcome, family!) when I'm struggling to feel productive with my writing. There's tangible evidence, at least until it's consumed, that I have done something useful with my time, and relief that it's a repeatable, predictable process. *Procrastibaking*.

At the outset, it may seem like one of the toughest parts about getting up at 5 a.m. for a 4% fix is the literal act of getting up. That can be true, but in my experience the larger hurdle to overcome is this: getting out of your own way. We are so good at putting up our own roadblocks, at being the cog in the wheel. At convincing ourselves with our mental loop of negative chatter that it will be *too difficult, too complicated, altogether too much, and so easier to not bother, really*. Far better to simply avoid it, or even better, to bake a lemon loaf, because when has a piece of sunshine cake failed to bring joy?

What does this look like, getting in our own way? I can give you a perfect example from a recent morning I had, when I was supposed to be working on a piece of writing that was being stubborn and moody.

- Wake up at 4:40 a.m.

- Make coffee, but then decide to check Twitter while coffee brews. *Roadblock #1*.

- Twenty minutes later, at 5 a.m., pour second cup of coffee and close Twitter. Friend texts me to check in. I decide it's urgent that I respond, despite the nature of her text being the opposite of urgent. *Roadblock #2*.

- Fifteen minutes later, finally open the document. Stare at it while I finish my coffee, then realize the dog is staring longingly at me for his morning biscuit. Put laptop to the side and fetch him his treat. *Roadblock #3.*

- Pour another coffee. Hungry now, so I rummage through the fridge. Could have an easy-to-grab yogurt, but instead decide some scrambled eggs would really hit the spot. *Roadblock #4.*

- Now it's 5:30 a.m. I'm full and well-caffeinated; the dog is happy and back to sleep. But I'm not sure what I want to write, so I stare at the blank screen a bit longer, hoping for inspiration. I tell myself I'm *thinking*, which is something writers call "work"—and sometimes *it is*, but oftentimes it's simple procrastination in costume.

- Finally, at around 6 a.m., I buckle down. However, I've lost that first sliver of cake that feeds my creative endeavours. Like a Dustbuster on high speed, I sucked up my time thanks to a handful of avoidable roadblocks and completely got in my own way.

Technology is another roadblock that has tricked us into thinking we're being much more productive than we probably are. During a *Better Life Lab* podcast on the topic of busyness, the issue of email came up, and the question about whether it's a wonderful invention that helps us stay connected, or an evil, time-draining innovation that has screwed up our priorities.

It was described like this: when we get physical mail delivered, it's easy for us to sort through what we need to pay attention to—the hydro bill and tax letter are important, but the pizza flyer and credit card application are fine for the recycling bin. The challenge with email is that *every* message appearing in your inbox carries with it, at least initially, a high level of importance. So if we get 100 emails a day, we're forced to operate as though each one deserves our utmost attention and focus. *Time-wasting roadblock.*

Admittedly, it can at times seem impossible to restrict these roadblocks. Some days I reflect and realize, perhaps, the roadblocks were present because I needed the morning off. Even from a project I felt completely engaged in and motivated by—we all need breaks. And, in case you need to hear it, *a rest is not the same thing as quitting.* However, if one day of rest turns into three, and then a dozen, you've likely entered giving-up territory and it is time to re-evaluate—without judgment or guilt—your project and your commitment to it.

Getting out of your own way should be simple. You are at the controls and have the greatest say about what you do— or don't do—each and every day. Yet, when you consider the vast number of things that can be standing between you and accomplishing something—fear, anxiety, ego, pressures, distractions, uncertainty, your inner critic, banana bread, to name a few—it can feel like someone else is driving the bus. Which then makes you the back-seat driver, and no one wants or needs one of those. Time to take back the steering wheel, however that looks for you. In my house, it means fewer banana bread loaves.

ADULTING IS EXHAUSTING

There is more to life than increasing its speed.
—Mahatma Gandhi

I f you find yourself decision-weary by 6 p.m.—having spent the day putting out fires, managing household or work tasks, making choices about everything from what to wear to what to make for dinner—you can in part blame a small section of your brain, near your temple, called the anterior cingulate cortex (ACC). Like the fuel tank of a car putting in miles on a road trip, the ACC gets depleted throughout the day with every decision you make. Particularly if those decisions are higher risk, like a work decision where the outcome will have a significant impact. Basically, the more important the outcome is, the more the decision-making depletes your ACC. If you find yourself faced with a day full of challenging decisions, you may also find yourself wishing it was bedtime by around 5 p.m.

A quick online search for the number of decisions the average adult makes in a given day yields a variety of (non-scientific, but widely shared) figures, with 35,000 being a common one. Actual science, via a 2007 Cornell University study by Wansink and Sobal, took a narrower approach and found that approximately 250 of our daily decisions are around food alone. These seem like mind-boggling numbers, don't they? Though if you begin adding up your daily decisions, it becomes more obvious how one could arrive at this number.

- Should I have that second cup of coffee?

- Should I let the dog out now or after I shower?

- Can we count olives in my kid's lunch box as a vegetable today?

- Will I have time to shoot off that email before I have to leave for the train?

These are all quick little decisions that require a miniscule amount of consciousness to make, but nonetheless, your ACC loses some fuel in the process.

- There's a snowstorm forecasted . . . should I risk a longer drive or take the train?

88

Bye-bye to some more decision-making fuel.

- What can I offer that irate client so it's a win-win all around?

There goes a portion of your ACC's fuel once again, and this time rather than a trickle it's a flood, because this is an important client and so the decision requires more effort. Unfortunately, when your ACC runs out of its fuel stores, you start making mistakes, which is also roughly when you start to feel that weariness, where making one more decision may just send you to bed for days.

This "adulting" weariness has a name: decision fatigue. And it helps support the idea of that first hour of your morning being ideal to work on something requiring focus and attention. At that time of day, we are fresh-brained and our ACCs are humming along, the fuel tank full and not yet depleted by the day's decisions.

Many of us are suffering from decision fatigue on a near daily basis. However, there are strategies you can apply to help reduce the number of decisions you have to make each day, salvaging the fuel you'd otherwise be draining from your ACC tank. One is to effectively schedule many of your decisions ahead of time, and with consistency: meal preparation (think batch cooking, food and meal delivery, weekly digital recipe planning); prepaying bills online or signing up for automatic withdrawals; scheduling laundry and dry cleaning pickup and drop-off; delegating the task of what to wear to an algorithm that chooses from your closet for you.

Some people even employ "capsule wardrobes" as a way to remove these daily clothing decisions. Similar in concept to school uniforms, a capsule wardrobe limits your outfit choices to only a few, making your life infinitely easier each morning as you decide what to wear. It's an idea embraced by many well-known business leaders and even a former U.S. president: Steve Jobs, a founder of Apple, apparently wore the same thing every day (black turtleneck, jeans, runners); Mark Zuckerberg, the man behind Facebook, has a similar daily look (grey T-shirt, jeans, runners); and President Barack Obama supposedly owned only navy-blue suits so he didn't have to take up precious brain space (which needed to be reserved for critical decisions, with high-level consequences) picking out his daily outfits.

Which brings me back to our ACC and how it relates to getting up and embracing a 4% fix. We've been talking about focus, distractions, procrastination, and how we can get more of the first and less of the others, and this next part is really about combining all that learning and understanding into one clear approach. Essentially, the message (and your ACC will thank you for this) is, *Do the most important thing first.* Oh, and do it in the morning, because science shows us willpower is strongest in the a.m., and because willpower is a finite resource, it *will* deplete as the day goes on. This is particularly true if creativity is required for your project . . . and let's be honest here, what project doesn't require at least an iota of creative energy?

Right after we wake up, our prefrontal cortex is at its most active and we have greater connection between the various parts of our brain, which is why we have better access to our creativity after we've slept (conversely, the analytical parts of our brain become more active as the day progresses). It also won't surprise anyone that after a good night's sleep your mind is fresher—and your ACC fuel tank is full—which is why a 5 a.m.-ish wake-up, while alarmingly early to some, is worth considering if you want to access valuable brain space and time. However, one thing you want to make sure you don't do is to overtax your decision-making abilities too early. Try to stay off social media, for example, which is a sure-fire way to get to the decision fatigue stage much more quickly, as scrolling through tweets forces your brain to have to decide what to focus on in rapid succession.

Willpower and focus don't kick in simply because you want them to. It's easy to confuse hoping for the best with doing your best when it comes to removing distractions, beefing up willpower, and preventing yourself from "distraction procrastination." If you save that 4% fix until later in the day, or until the evening, once all of your daily to-do boxes have been ticked off and managed, you might find yourself with a big fat zero on your ACC gas tank. Which means you'll likely get easily diverted and then promise yourself you'll simply shut everything down and start fresh the next day. Wash, rinse, repeat . . . a reliable way to ensure it never happens.

I laughed out loud when a post came across my Instagram feed the other day, essentially commenting how a task this person had been avoiding for six months ended up taking only 15 minutes, and noting that she would, of course, learn nothing from this. It was easy to relate—I have a list of tasks that fit that description—but it also reminded me about the power of choosing to spend that first hour of my day the way I do.

There will always be things that have to get done, some

more urgently than others, and unless we plan a worldwide revolt, we won't be giving up our addiction to busyness or productivity anytime soon. Nor is the need to continue making many daily decisions going to go away for the majority of us. Which means we need a plan, a commitment, an alarm clock . . . and the desire to take back control over our time. Adulting is exhausting, ACC-taxing, and quite frankly, some days, utter bullshit. But the choice to invest in yourself can be a no-brainer.

NO WIGGLE ROOM

Life shrinks or expands in proportion to one's courage.
—Anaïs Nin

Children, train schedules or long commutes, work responsibilities . . . all these can feel as though they're conspiring against you finding time for yourself. But what about when the bottom falls out of your life? What happens when you literally don't have time to take a deep breath?

Before March 17, 2018, I thought I had already experienced "when your life goes to shit." More than once. When I was diagnosed with cancer, for one. That was pretty shitty. Then when I had a newborn and it was my job, all of a sudden, to keep another human alive. That might have been harder than the cancer, quite honestly. However, neither situation compared to when my husband crash landed—on skis—in a mogul field on one of our winter ski weekends. He's an expert skier—we've both been on skis since we could walk—and nothing about that day, about that ski hill, about that particular run, should have spelled disaster for him. Yet, disaster it was.

For about 30 seconds after he stopped cartwheeling across the hill in a hurricane of snow I thought he might be dead. He wasn't moving. Then I worried about his spine, his neck, his head. Thankfully, all those things were okay. But the reason he couldn't move as he lay on that hill was because he had broken half his body, and then some. The list of injuries was staggering: dislocated shoulder, one arm broken from shoulder to wrist, a blown-out knee, and a broken right hand that required surgery. What all this meant was that he had quite a long recovery ahead of him. And with bilateral casts on his arms for a number of weeks, he was completely dependent on others.

When I was diagnosed with cancer, Adam was the one who took care of me. He's an excellent dad and partner. But suddenly, when faced with one of the greatest challenges of my adult life—being a caregiver to my husband—I didn't have the partner I'd had through my other challenges. We had a hospital bed in our bedroom. Around-the-clock medical care was required, including middle-of-the-night painkillers, and wound care, and feeding, and everything in between. In some ways, it felt like I had a newborn again—I was solo parenting, exhausted, and full of worry because we weren't sure how well he would recover. Plus, I was only a couple of months out from my fourth novel being published.

Luckily, we did have some help. Our families stepped in wherever they could. Friends delivered food and support at regular intervals. Regardless, it was a very hard few months. During those months, and for the first time since I had started writing fiction, my 5 a.m. sessions ceased. There was no writing being done that wasn't absolutely mandatory. I was often up early, but I had a million other things I had to do to keep my day on track. However, the wheels did not fall off the bus. At least, not off *every* bus. I didn't miss deadlines. While I fell behind on daily word counts, I didn't fall behind on projects. How? Simply, I was ahead of schedule when his accident happened. I had been getting up at 5 a.m. for long enough that I had banked the benefits of my early-rising habit. Then, when my life went to shit, I cashed in.

For anyone who's fairly sure that the category I like to call "No Wiggle Room" (which includes kids, commutes, jobs, etc.) will screw with your ability to use that first hour differently than you do now, let me assure you: it most definitely will. You can count on it.

If you want to learn to play an instrument, but you also want your family to continue sleeping, you might have to get resourceful. Or, if you've always wanted to run a 10K, but the only time you can train is around the same time you need to be on your way to work, you'll have a tough time achieving that goal.

Making this change to your schedule takes more than wishing for it to happen—or for me to magically manifest the day's 25th hour for you. It would be fantastic if I could do that, but I fear many people would use it to do more work, which completely defeats the purpose of a magic hour. While

I can't predict where exactly you'll get that extra time, I *can* help you figure out how to find your own 4% fix.

Let's talk kids for a moment. Particularly the really young ones and the tweens and teenagers who are so packed into activities that you've become more chauffeur than parent. Wiggle room can be hard to come by. When my daughter was a baby (and toddler), I would try to remember what exactly I had done all day. I had been busy. But doing what, I couldn't say, except that I was busy being a mother. If that's the stage you're in, you may not be able to find a consistent hour every day. Perhaps your child is still napping twice a day (my kid never did, but I have heard rumours that some do), and one of those naps is time you can recapture for yourself, even if not every day, maybe a couple of times a week. All you need is a starting point, and a willingness to give it a try.

Take a week and have a look at where you have consistent breaks. My daughter was a very early riser, but she was in bed by 6 p.m. for her "first" sleep—until she woke up at 11 p.m. for a snack, then back to bed. I could reliably count on an hour or so in the early evening that I could claim as my own. Once the pattern was predictable, I coveted that hour. Sometimes I read a book, sometimes I worked on a magazine pitch, sometimes I took a long, hot shower, and sometimes I had a nap. But it was an hour I *could* claim, and so I did.

When kids are older and locked into a zillion programs, there's much shuffling that happens. However, you might find yourself with an hour or more sitting in an arena or at a gymnastics practice or in a coffee shop close to wherever your kid is doing whatever it is they do a few times a week. Rather than dropping my daughter off and going home, I would set myself up at the gym (or in my car, if that was the only place I could sit) with my laptop. Now, if writing isn't your thing and let's say, to use an example above, learning to play an instrument is, you may have a harder time being so nimble. However, why not check out if there are any lessons offered nearby, so while your kid does their thing, you can do yours? This isn't about setting up the perfect scenario, it's about figuring out how to steal that hour back for yourself—even if you sit in a freezing-cold car, fingerless mittens on and hot tea beside you, so you can get your 500-word-count goal completed while your kid does piano lessons.

The same will be true for work and commutes and other such responsibilities with zero wiggle room. So, similar to the above scenario, it might be tough to find an hour a day that isn't already spoken for. Again, let's forgo perfection. This is not a race, and if you can carve out even one hour, once a week, for that 4% fix, you will make progress.

Of course, if you don't believe you can make it work, you absolutely won't make it work. Funny how that works, eh?

I'll say it again—once more for those in the back: this is not about rigidity. There is nothing enjoyable about trying to stick with something that is making other aspects of your life miserable. Perhaps there are certain months when adding anything to the schedule feels impossible. Maybe it's the kind of thing you can make work during the week, or only on the weekends. Consistency counts, but that doesn't mean it has to be every single day of every single week for you to benefit from harnessing the power of that 4% fix.

THAT NATURAL FEELING

Start where you are. Use what you have. Do what you can.
—ARTHUR ASHE

B *rain Games* is a National Geographic series that examines the realities of human perception, with fun and fascinating experiments that pair regular people with illusionists, magicians, scientists, and medical experts. It's one of our favourite shows to watch as a family, and in one particular episode they showcased an experiment that proved how flexible and malleable our brains are. In it, a professional BMX rider named Charles was asked to stop riding his regular bike and instead ride a "backwards" bike for two weeks.

The backwards bike seemed impossible to ride, and *was* for many who tested it out, providing much entertainment for the crowd, before Charles was sent home with it. In order to turn right with the backwards bike, you had to turn the handlebars left, and vice versa to go to the left, which is counterintuitive and not typically how a regular bike (or car, or boat, or skidoo, or anything with a steering-wheel mechanism) works. Even when Charles—a professional biker—got on the backwards bike for the first time, it was a gong show. He looked like he had never ridden a bike before. But, after two weeks of riding only the backwards bike, something amazing happened: Charles had managed to remodel the neural pathways in his brain through practice and was able to ride the backwards bike seamlessly. Way to go, Charles!

But because this is television and we needed another plot twist, the *Brain Games* host brought out Charles's old bike—the one he rode professionally—and it was a repeat scenario of two weeks earlier. He wobbled and bobbled and couldn't make his regular bike, the one he was an expert at riding, stay straight. I'm not sure how Charles felt about that part of the experiment, as the show cut at that point (hopefully Charles got his riding legs back soon after), but it was an entertaining yet clear example of how our brain can (and will) learn something new . . . if given the opportunity to do so.

This mechanism of neuroplasticity—essentially how experiences reorganize neural pathways in our brains—happens throughout our lives and is affected not only by stages of development but also by our environments and our learning. There will be a point when the thing you're doing—even if it's a brand-new something—will shift from feeling unnatural to becoming more of a habit, as long as you're consistent. Because with consistency, like riding a backwards bike for a couple of weeks, the behaviour is reinforced, and new neural pathways are created. Unfortunately, this is true for both good behaviours and not-so-good ones. It applies whether you're trying to create a 5 a.m. wake-up habit to uncover time to yourself, or whether you're forming a new salt-and-vinegar kettle chip addiction during your global pandemic isolation weeks—both of which I can attest to from personal experience.

Dr. Ann Graybiel, a professor and researcher at the Massachusetts Institute of Technology (MIT), is an expert on the neurophysiology of how habits form. And her research with rats helps us understand why habits can be both notoriously hard to break (especially "bad" habits, like smoking) and also crazy easy to resume (again, a nod to anyone who has ever tried to quit smoking). There are critical neural activity patterns in our brains that change when habits are formed, then change again when we break those habits. But interestingly, if something happens to resurrect one of those broken habits— say, a smoker gets stressful news and then finds herself out for dinner with a friend who smokes—those original patterns re-emerge and voila: good or bad, the habit is yours again.

This is both excellent and terrible news, depending on the habit in question. But let's think about this from the standpoint of getting up early, even 5 a.m. early, for a 4% fix. We know we can create a habit or routine with practice, thanks to our brain's ability to form new pathways. Thereby, we can also deduce that by consistently setting an early alarm and getting out of bed, we can create a new pathway where the behaviour (early rising) will not only begin to feel easier . . . it will feel downright natural. Essentially, you're retraining your brain—and those neural activity patterns—and as a result, solidifying a brand-new habit with tons of potential.

At first you will feel a lot like Charles trying to ride the backwards bike. You will want to go back to your original bike (a more civilized wake-up time) and will have to work hard to see the point of switching your 7 a.m. bike for a 5 a.m. version. But if you stick with it and allow those new neural pathways to get laid down, it won't be too long before 5 a.m. doesn't feel that different from 7 a.m. or later. Then, when you try to go back to sleeping in, it will feel entirely uncomfortable and surprisingly challenging to stay in bed so long.

If the idea of being awake at 5 a.m. still feels prickly at best and earth-shatteringly painful at worst, not to worry—I'm here for you. We have entered the world of high expectations with no proof yet of the thing's success. Exploiting that first hour of your day via a 4% fix could be everything you imagined . . . or one heck of a crash-and-burn situation. As we talked about earlier, the good news is that most of us have plenty of experience with being a newbie; whether it involves an academic endeavour, an exercise program, the first day of a job or taking up an artistic hobby, we have all felt the excitement, trepidation, and wonderful sense of possibility that come with new beginnings. Yet despite all of this practice, new starts continue to bring discomfort. So much is unknown! Will this shift lead to something significant and life-altering or be discarded into the "better luck next time" bucket we all have?

Like nearly everything else I've set out to do for the first time, getting up at 5 a.m. did not come naturally. But committing to that first-4% slice of my day *did change my life.* If that sounds dramatic, good—that was on purpose. It's with full confidence that I declare I would not be the writer I am today if not for those early, early mornings. The self-identified night owls in the crowd may find this impossible to believe, but 5 a.m. was—and continues to be—my current version of the "me first" oxygen mask scenario.

However, when you've been doing something for a while—long enough that it becomes second nature—you can lose perspective. I rarely need an alarm anymore, as my body clock and circadian rhythms have adjusted. I also no longer stumble around bleary-eyed for the rest of the day. So when people ask how the f*ck I get up so early, day after day, year after year, when I don't *have* to, it can be hard to remember what the big deal is. I mean, sure, I get that it's early. But in my world, it's also *normal* and perfectly natural to be up before the sun. And since I go to bed earlier than everyone who asks me the "How?" question, I can also get up earlier— the neural pathway is paved with asphalt at this point.

I understand this is simplistic, but that doesn't make it less true. I do set an alarm, even if I wake up before it goes off most days. But because I know it's set, I can relax when I head to bed. Then, the only thing I have to do at 5 a.m. is get out of bed, which puts into motion everything that follows.

As for the "That's great, but *what am I supposed to be doing* once I get out of bed?" issue, I bet your subconscious already has a couple of ideas brewing. Our brains have superpowers—I've already offered a couple of examples to back this up—and if you give your mind the tiniest bit of slack, you'll be amazed at all the great ideas that can flow into that newly created space.

But let's not forget the oxygen mask, or that delicious cake sliced into 24 pieces. None of this works if you're unwilling to commit to finding yourself *the time to make it work*. It doesn't have to all align right now; you just have to accept it won't feel natural at first and be okay with a touch of discomfort.

And perhaps most importantly, you need to be willing to gift yourself this one hour—4% of all the hours you have in a day—without guilt. Take care of yourself by taking care of your time.

MORNING LARKS AND NIGHT OWLS

A little insomnia is not without its value in making us appreciate sleep, in throwing a ray of light upon that darkness.
—MARCEL PROUST

There's this great GIF that floats around social media every now and again showing two small dogs, one standing by its food bowl in a hallway and the other racing at top speed back and forth while the non-moving dog watches, her glance shifting between the camera and the sprinting dog. Usually there's a caption attached, saying something to the effect of "Morning people versus everyone else." (If you want to watch the original video, search under "Dog with too much energy runs back and forth while sister eats breakfast"—you won't regret it.)

I laughed—hard—the first time I saw it, and promptly sent it to my husband, who is a trained early riser like me but falls into the camp of wishing he was still in bed most days. This video perfectly captures the annoyance so many people seem to have for those who choose to rise early, when we don't have to, and with an obnoxious amount of vim and vigour. But it also highlights the stark differences between the morning larks and night owls in the crowd. Of course, if we were to look at the other end of the day, late in the evening, that same early bird might be zonked out and already drooling on her pillow while the night owl is just warming up.

Benjamin Franklin famously said, "Early to bed, early to rise makes a man healthy, wealthy, and wise," which certainly seems to favour the morning larks of the world. This statement, however, has been debated in recent years, and some studies show that night owls (those going to bed after 11 p.m. and rising after 8 a.m.) *may* in fact be slightly more intelligent and wealthier.

However, if you're what's considered a morning lark (in bed before 11 p.m., up before 8 a.m.), studies show you are likely more persistent, have fewer bad habits, procrastinate less, and overall are happier than those going to bed late and rising late. But before you decide to switch your sleep and wake patterns depending on which of these traits is most appealing at the present moment, it's important to note that most of these studies looked at only small samples of participants. The "happier" study had fewer than 1,000 people involved, and the one that found higher intelligence in the evening folk looked at results from just 420 participants.

It should also be noted that most of us do not fall into rigid lark or owl categories, either. Like my husband, who on paper looks like a true morning person (he's up before 6 a.m. most days of the week) but would probably have more night-owl tendencies if he were able to manipulate his schedule differently. I am certainly in the lark camp today, but there was a time not so long ago when I self-identified as a night owl, thank you very much.

Dr. Michael Breus, the "Sleep Doctor" and author, has taken the two-category "lark" and "owl" labels and expanded them into four distinct (but still animal-themed) chronotypes. A chronotype is your personal biological clock, and the reason why you find it easy (or not) to bounce out of bed in the morning or to stay up so late everyone else has gone to bed. It's also responsible for how alert you feel, when you do your best focused work throughout the day, and how easily you fall asleep or how affected you are by jet lag or time changes.

There are four chronotypes, according to Dr. Breus:

- **Lions**, who get up between 4:30 and 5 a.m., represent about 15% of the population and have Type A features to their personalities.

- **Bears**, who get up when the sun rises and go to bed when the moon shows up, make up about 55% of us. They are generally easier-going than Lions and tend to have decent sleep habits.

- **Wolves** only make up 15% of the population and are the night owls of the bunch, staying up much later than the rest of us. They tend to be more introverted and creative types.

- **Dolphins**, the remaining 15% of us, are "rough sleepers"—similar to Lions in that they wake up early, but they tend to be insomniacs and have a lot of anxiety. They can be quite productive, but they don't sleep well, according to Dr. Breus.

When I did the quiz in Dr. Breus's bestselling 2016 book, *The Power of When: Discover Your Chronotype—and the Best Time to Eat Lunch, Ask for a Raise, Have Sex, Write a Novel, Take Your Meds, and More*, I came out as a Lion, which definitely fits with how I structure my days and when I'm at my best.

Now, night owls who dream of tackling creative endeavours with any extra time you can find, listen up: Dr. Breus, through his research and work with patients, says the best time for someone with late-night tendencies (like owls or, in his classification system, Wolves) to work creatively is *first thing in the morning*. Early enough that you're still a bit sleepy and fuzzy-brained. Focused time is still going to be easiest to harness when you're most alert, so later in the evening, but the ability to think outside the box and be creative, versus analytical, is going to be best in the early morning for the night owl folks.

One final note about timing and creativity that is relevant if you're a night owl struggling in a morning lark world, or if you remain in denial that 5 a.m. *may* be the right time of day for you, after all: in Daniel H. Pink's book *When: The Scientific Secrets of Perfect Timing*, he talks about the "inspiration paradox"—the idea that innovation and creativity are greatest when we are *not* at our best, at least according to our natural circadian rhythms. So if you're a night owl, the "thrives after 11 p.m." sort, bursting with energy in the evening and feeling sluggish in the morning, the earlier hours of the day would be best for your creative work. If nothing else, at that time of day those voices that like to tell us "this is not possible" may still be asleep, so good news for your creativity!

Flip it around for the larks (the Lions and Dolphins, but presumably not the Bears, who seem to be in the "sweet spot" when it comes to sleep), Dr. Breus says. According to *The Power of When*, the best time for me—as a Lion and a lark—to write a novel is in the evening. And the best time to edit said novel is in the morning. This is exactly the opposite of how I've written all my novels to date. So, while my brain's ability to focus on a creative task like writing might peak later in the day, I have developed an early-morning habit that means I can write—or edit, for that matter—at 5 a.m. My life simply won't allow me to find the focused time I need after dinner, because that's when I'm heavily into kid activities and, quite honestly, the wind-down before bed. Not to say I've never done it (in fact, I wrote many of this book's chapters while watching my daughter's evening trampoline training sessions), but it feels harder than it does at 5 a.m., likely because of the aforementioned asphalt neural pathway.

Labels are effective only if they make your life easier or less complicated or provide some sort of benefit, so if the above information intrigues you and makes you think, "I wonder if there's anything to that," fantastic. But much like the waistband of the pair of pants you sport to your family's Thanksgiving dinner, it might be best to wear your sleep category label loosely as well. Try it on for size, take a look at how alert and focused you feel in the morning or evening based on whether you self-identify as a lark or owl, and then do *the opposite* of what you're currently doing. For *Seinfeld* fans, this will be similar to the episode where George Costanza decided to do the opposite of what he would normally do—including sleeping on the job and telling a woman he wanted to date that he was broke and still lived with his parents—and had unbelievable, hilarious success as a result.

It's possible you'll hate this particular experiment. And I know the owls of the bunch are thinking they'll hate it the *most*, having to get up much earlier than normal. As someone who feels her best in the pre-dawn hours, the thought of staying up late and having to do more than sit on the couch and stare sleepily into space makes me grumpy.

If you're wondering if you can change your chronotype or biological clock, here's the deal: according to Breus, we actually move between chronotypes depending on our age. For example, most toddlers are Lions, as anyone who has one at home can attest to, as are many seniors, while teenagers tend to trend to the Wolf category. But to shift intentionally from being a Lion to being a Bear, for example, isn't easy, which is why many people struggle through school and work if their biological clocks don't match their schedules. Being a true night owl in a morning lark job, with a 9 a.m. or earlier start to your day, means you're consistently working against your natural sleep cycles. This is one of the reasons we drink so much coffee, says Breus: we're trying to use caffeine to help us adjust our biological clocks (this is not a permanent solution, by the way).

You can, however, hack your biological clock with a bit of effort and planning. If you want to wake up earlier and, beyond that, be more productive first thing in the morning, you need to move your to-bed time forward in small increments and adjust your wake-up time by a comparable margin. It's not much different from dealing with jet lag, which most of us have experienced at one point or another.

The trick, though, is not to put yourself in a state of sleep deprivation, because even if doing so gives you that extra hour in the morning, if you've underslept, you will be miserable. Which is a crappy way to start your day and leads to bad moods and overall misery for everyone. Let's not do that to ourselves or to those we love (even if they are self-righteous, early-rising, Type A Lions), okay? Okay.

SLEEP: WHY WE NEED IT

It is a common experience that a problem difficult
at night is resolved in the morning after the committee
of sleep has worked on it.
—JOHN STEINBECK

I n 1965 a 17-year-old high school student, Randy Gardner, stayed awake for 264 hours (11 days) to see how he would fare without sleep. Not surprisingly, a host of awful things started to happen: on day 2, his eyes stopped focusing; by day 3, he was moody and uncoordinated, and had lost his ability to figure out what an object was through touch; and by day 11, he was struggling with short-term memory, became paranoid, and started hallucinating. Young Gardner apparently recovered without long-term consequences, but his 11-day experiment showed that sleep deprivation is about much more than simply feeling exhausted.

If we look way back into the history of sleep, we'll find that humans used to sleep about the same percentage of each day as we should now (about 30% of the day, or 8 slices of cake), but their sleep was segmented. Historian Roger Ekirch uncovered that our ancestors used to go to bed once it got dark, sleep for about four hours, then wake up for a while before settling into a "second sleep," which lasted another four hours. During this middle-of-the-night awake time, they would do things like read by candlelight, have sex, and quietly visit with one another. Basically, doing what many of us modern humans do *before* going to bed for the night.

This two-step system is called "biphasic sleep" and it seems to be the way we all slept up until the 1800s, when artificial illumination became widely available and affordable. This artificial light allowed people to move about safely after dark—and in a socially acceptable way, as back then the night hours were reserved for, ahem, less palatable activities—and as a result, our sleep habits changed. Then industrialization solidified the single sleep cycle as the social norm, as a fascination with productivity and a formalized workday structure was established. At this point it would have been considered "slothful" to loll about in the middle of the night.

Because our ancestors were constrained by the rising and setting of the sun, sleep deprivation was not the societal issue it has become today. Nowadays, if you want to stay up all night and never sleep again, there's likely an app for that . . . or at least a hundred different ways you can keep yourself occupied. Humans were never meant to be nocturnal, of course, but many of us are feeling the crunch of our responsibilities overtaking our rest time.

We've all been there and know that feeling: bone-deep exhaustion sucks. Not only is it an unpleasant state of being, it also carries dangerous health consequences and can feel like a dreaded roller-coaster ride you can't get off. And considering how vital sleep is to our well-being, we are terrible at getting enough of it. Russell Foster, a circadian neuroscientist who studies the sleep cycles of the brain, has said that if you live to age 90, you will have spent 32 years of your life sleeping. However, many of us are playing fast and free with our sleep schedules these days, with plenty of modern distractions making it harder to get the shut-eye we need. Overall, most adults are failing miserably at getting the recommended seven to nine hours per night.

Time for some hard health facts: If you sleep around five hours or less a night, you have a 50% increased chance of being obese. Sleep deprivation causes the hunger-stimulating hormone ghrelin to rise (and the hunger-controlling hormone leptin to fall), which the brain then reads as "I need carbohydrates"—particularly sugars. A study done by University of Pennsylvania researchers found that when participants were limited to four and a half hours of sleep a night for one week, they reported feeling more sad, angry, and stressed. And sustained stress—which comes from regular sleep deprivation—leads to lowered immunity. In a 2019 publication of *The Lancet Oncology*, night-shift work was classified as "probably carcinogenic to humans." Basically, according to Foster, sleep loss causes a heck of a lot more than just a mildly impaired brain—it is downright detrimental to your health.

Along with health issues, sleep deprivation can lead to other problems, such as "microsleep," which is when the brain forces sleep. Essentially, it's like a hard shutdown on your laptop or phone: there is no choice but to "go to sleep." It's uncontrollable, and it has been estimated that 31% of drivers microsleep—leading to the dreaded "falling asleep at the wheel" state. The National Highway Traffic Safety Administration in the U.S. found that in 2013 "drowsy driving" caused over 72,000 crashes, 44,000 injuries, and 600 deaths.

When you're sleep-deprived, you end up with mediocre memory, lowered creativity, increased impulsiveness, and overall poor judgment. If you have a tired brain, it *craves* things to wake it up: stimulants like caffeine and other "upper" drugs. But fuelling your awake state with these stimulants throughout the day means you can't fall asleep when evening arrives. This leads to the use of other drugs, such as alcohol, to try to induce sleepiness. But alcohol, while it can help to bridge the gap between the awake and sleep states, doesn't actually help with the biological process of sleep. That glass of wine simply sedates you, even harming some of the neural processing that goes on during memory consolidation and memory record.

When you're asleep the brain does not shut down; in fact, some areas of your brain are *more active* during sleep than they are during wakefulness. One of the structures that matters most to the sleep process is the hypothalamus, which, if you were to flip a brain upside down you'd find on its underside. There are a few critical structures nestled inside the hypothalamus, including our biological clock, which tells us when it's time to be asleep or awake. Essentially, this part of the brain sends messages to the brain stem, which then projects them forward and bathes the cortex (what we see as the wrinkly surface) with neurotransmitters, cueing the "rise and shine" signal to wake up.

So, by now I'm sure we're all on the same page: sleep is necessary, and it is complex. We know why we *need* to sleep, but what about why we sleep in the first place? Being able to stay up for 24 hours, without the negative consequences of sleep deprivation, would create quite a different world than the one we have now. But scientists can't actually come to a consensus about *why* we sleep, according to Foster. However, there are three ideas worth noting, he says. The first, *restoration*, is somewhat intuitive: all the stuff we deplete and burn out during the day, we restore and replace and rebuild during the night. The concept of restoration goes back to Aristotle and has gone in and out of fashion over the years. But what gives it momentum as an explanation for sleep is that research has shown that, within the brain, some genes get turned on *only* during sleep. And those genes are associated with restoration and metabolic pathways.

Next up: *energy conservation*. Basically, sleeping saves calories. The energy savings of sleep equals about 110 calories a night, which is equivalent to the caloric value of a banana. So really, that's not a lot of calories to be saving for such a complicated and demanding process as sleep.

Finally, some scientists believe we sleep for brain processing and memory consolidation. Sleep scientist and *Why We Sleep* author Matthew Walker explains that you need sleep after learning so you can hit the save button on those memories, but you also need sleep *before* learning. He compares the brain to a sponge that's dry and ready to soak everything up; in order for learning to take place, you must have a rested brain. Without sleep, the memory circuits of the brain become waterlogged, and you can't absorb new memories. However, it isn't just about laying down memory, recording it, and saving it. Sleep has also been shown to enhance our creativity, helping us find novel solutions to challenging problems.

Regardless of why we need it, sleep is not an indulgence. It's not to be managed casually, or without intention. Jessa Gamble, a writer and co-owner of the science blog *The Last Word on Nothing*, talks about how when people aren't influenced by unnatural light, they sleep twice a night—similar to the biphasic sleep patterns of the past. They go to bed around 8 p.m., sleep until midnight, have a "meditative" but awake-in-bed rest until around 2 a.m., and then fall back asleep until sunrise. She says that these people are so alert during the daytime, despite this awake break, they feel they're experiencing true awareness for first time in their lives.

So, poor sleep can make us sick and stressed, and potentially lead to risky and rash decisions. But according to professor and sleep coach Dan Gartenberg, it is also a drain on our empathy. Gartenberg says that because sleep deprivation makes us more sensitive to our own pain, we subsequently have a hard time relating to what others might be going through.

Sleep may be complicated, but it is critical. And while this chapter might give you nightmares (sorry about that), rest easy, because next up we'll talk about *how* you can get a better night's sleep.

SLEEP: HOW IT WORKS AND HOW TO GET IT

A good laugh and a long sleep are the best cures in the doctor's book.
—IRISH PROVERB

When our daughter was a baby, my husband and I came up with a nighttime strategy intended to allow for maximum rest. Regardless, it was never enough, because newborns operate on a 24-hour clock, and 3 a.m. is as good a time as any to be *wide awake* and ready to party. We were so sleep deprived I'm not sure how we were functioning. But we were determined, if perhaps naive (she was our first and only), and so believed we had cracked the code. I would wake up to feed her, and then my husband would change her diaper while I went back to bed to reboot for the next round of fun. The dog would sit watch with the both of us, and then go back to sleep when my husband did.

One night, after her midnight feeding, I called to my husband that it was time for diaper changing. *Silence.* I tried again. Nothing, still. The dog, who was wise to our routine by now, trotted back to our bedroom and stood at the door, waiting for my husband to realize it was his turn. Finally, after I shouted one more time, he appeared bleary-eyed in the hallway—in boxers and with his bedside table lamp in hand, having clearly yanked the cord from the wall—and yelled, "What?" When I repeated it was diaper-changing time, he just stared at me and then slowly said, "I do not understand the words coming out of your mouth." The dog looked back and forth at us, and I started laughing. My husband had been sleepwalking, the many nights of broken rest finally catching up with him, and so I sent him back to bed with the lamp and the dog, and changed her diaper myself.

How can you tell if you're not getting enough sleep? If in order to get moving in the morning you need an alarm clock and stimulants (like caffeine), *and* you feel grumpy, irritable, and lethargic, chances are you're not sleeping enough. We've already discussed a couple of tips and tricks to improve bedtime and the likelihood of falling asleep (reducing caffeine after 2 p.m. and banishing artificial light, particularly blue-light devices, from the bedroom). But before we talk more about *how* to get more sleep, we need to understand what we're working with.

There are three stages of sleep: light sleep, rapid eye movement (REM), and deep sleep (or slow-wave sleep). In light sleep, your body is essentially preparing for the deeper sleep coming next: your breathing and heartbeat slow, and your muscles relax. In REM sleep, your brainwaves are very similar to those during your awake phase. As well, your heart rate and blood pressure increase, and your eyes move back and forth rapidly. This stage is when you dream. But our deep-sleep brainwaves are quite different. They are long-burst waves, called delta waves, that we need to facilitate learning and for our cells and bodies to recover. During deep sleep, your heart rate and breathing slow to their lowest points during the entire sleep cycle.

While it's assumed that both REM and deep sleep are required for memory consolidation, that rested feeling you have when you wake up—it's all due to deep sleep. So, we can simplify the sleep stages in this way: deep sleep is important for our bodies; REM sleep is important for our brains.

Let's move a bit deeper into the brain, into the hypothalamus, where our biological clock is located. This internal clock seems to be timed to the rising and setting of the sun. If we were able to wake up with the rising of the sun, here's what would happen: as our eyes register that it's light out, our optic nerves send a message to the nerve cells in the hypothalamus. With the relaying of this message to the hypothalamus, sleep-related processes that wake us up begin: our body temperature rises and melatonin levels begin to drop.

We then tend to be at our cognitive best (most alert) in the late morning. While our strongest desire to sleep is between 2 and 4 a.m., the hour between 2 and 3 p.m. comes in a close second. That afternoon slump you're feeling? It's biological. And this will cause the nappers out there to rejoice, because this desire for a mid-afternoon catnap suggests they are a natural part of our body's rhythms and rest cycles. As the day progresses, there is one more period of alertness, and then our bodies and brains start preparing for slumber. Our organs shift into low gear, melatonin levels begin to rise, and our body temperatures start to drop. Essentially, the opposite of what happens when sunlight hits our optic nerves. Which brings me to the dilemma for many of us: our modern schedules don't correlate with sunrise and sunset any longer, and as a result we're constantly fighting against our biological clocks.

What's interesting, however, is that you don't even need to *see* the sun rise and set for this process to work. In scientist Michel Siffre's chronobiology work, he found that if you spend a significant portion of time isolated from clocks, natural light, or any other clues about time of day, your body continues to stay true to its internal clock. He did find that rather than a 24-hour cycle, people in these isolation studies operated more on a 24.5-hour daily cycle, and in his own case (he spent two months alone in a cave in 1962, and then three months in 1972), he would at times be awake for 36 hours and then sleep for 12 hours.

The problems begin when we start messing with our circadian rhythms by introducing artificial light and stimulants, both of which confuse our internal clocks and make our sleep cycles go haywire. Now, the "how *to*." Specifically, how can we change our environments and habits to get the best night's sleep possible?

- **Create a "power down" ritual at bedtime:** Remove all devices from the bedroom at least an hour before you go to sleep. Blue-light-emitting devices in particular need to be banished. I use

my phone as an alarm clock, but along with setting it to Night Shift mode from 7 p.m. to 7 a.m.,
which shifts the display colours to the warmer
end of the spectrum (read: reduces blue light), I
also put it on Do Not Disturb as soon as I head to
bed. Another suggestion to power down: don't
put a television in the bedroom. I remember my
family doctor once saying that bedrooms should
be only for sleep and another thing that begins
with the letter *s*. If you aren't one of those lucky
people who can close their eyes and fall straight
to sleep, reading (a physical book or an e-reader
that doesn't emit blue light) or using a meditation
app can help you transition to a sleepier state.

- **Make a sleep cave:** Both light and temperature
affect our sleep. One theory about why people
used to be less sleep-deprived is that nights were
inevitably cooler (thermostats allow our homes to
maintain a constant temperature), and a lowered
body temperature is one of the physiological processes involved in falling asleep. If we keep our
bedrooms too warm (the ideal temperature for
sleeping is between 18 and 21 degrees Celsius),
our bodies can't naturally cool down enough to
send us into deep slumber. Along with keeping
a lower temperature, you also want to make your
room as dark as possible, to avoid any ambient
light making its way to your optic nerves and
screwing with your sleep cycles.

- **Skip the afternoon latte (or make it decaf):** This may be obvious to most, but caffeine is a stimulant, and so consuming caffeinated beverages or foods after about 2 p.m. is a bad idea if you want to get to bed at a reasonable time.

- **Exercise, but with a caveat:** This is another one of those areas around sleep that continues to be researched, because while scientists believe exercise can help with sleep, they aren't exactly certain why. While aerobic exercise releases endorphins in the body, which can help wakefulness, research does show that moderate exercise decreases insomnia and increases the amount of deep sleep you get. However, exercising too close to bedtime can have the opposite effect as the brain deals with the wake-me-up endorphins.

- **Be consistent:** In Matthew Walker's book, *Why We Sleep*, his message about regularity is an important one. Walker says we need to go to bed at the same time and wake up at the same time every day. "Sleep is a non-negotiable, biological necessity," he says, and it doesn't bend to our preference to perhaps stay up much (much) later on the weekend.

- **Consider strategic napping:** Back when we first started dating, my husband tried to get me to appreciate the midday nap. I don't understand napping. Falling asleep in the middle of the afternoon? "Just relax, close your eyes, and fall asleep," he said. *But . . . how?* My body—and mind—knew it was only 12:30 p.m. Lunchtime! "I just don't need to sleep during the day," I said. Adam stared at me as though I had announced something unfathomable. "It isn't about *need*," he replied. "It's about want." When our daughter was born—a non-napper if I've ever known one—he would give me a pointed look as we tried every which way to get her to sleep at midday, and say, "Well, I guess she comes by it honestly." However, for the nappers in the crowd, we can look to Daniel H. Pink (author of *When*) for some good news. He says science tells us naps are valuable, but there is a rule for maximizing their benefits: the optimal length of a nap is 10 to 20 minutes. More than that, and you risk waking sluggish and cotton-headed. Pink also shares a way to boost the energy you can feel from a midday nap, employing a napping method he calls a "nappuccino": consume something with 200 milligrams of caffeine (so, one cup of coffee) immediately before your nap, then when you get up 20 minutes later, you'll enjoy both the benefits of a short rest and the jolt of caffeine (which takes about 25 minutes to move through your bloodstream).

- **Hack your circadian rhythm, in a helpful way:** Hate jet lag? (Who doesn't?) Starting a new job with a shift in work hours? Want to wake up at 5 a.m. to get an hour back for yourself? To adjust your sleep hours, the biggest tool at your disposal is light, or lack thereof. As we know, when it's dark outside, your brain naturally signals to your body to release melatonin, the sleep hormone. When it's light outside, your brain sends a signal to cut off the melatonin supply, making you feel more awake. To shift your circadian rhythm earlier, dim the lights in your home an hour before bedtime to prepare yourself for sleep. As soon as that early alarm goes off, turn on as many lights as you can to simulate a bright, sunny morning. Your circadian rhythm responds well to light cues, but other aspects of your daily life can influence it as well. For instance, the time of day you eat can speed up or delay your internal clock. If you shift your breakfasts, lunches, and dinners to later in the day, this may also move your body's internal clock back, making a later bedtime feel more natural.

Research continues, and if we know anything, it's that we don't fully understand the intricacies of sleep. What we *do* know, however, is how our well-being suffers when we don't get enough of it. None of us needs a massive body of research to realize sleep is directly linked to how we feel—physically, mentally, and emotionally. So let's circle back to the beginning, where I said getting a 4% fix is not about sleep deprivation. There's little benefit and zero enjoyment in serving yourself that first piece of cake if you fall asleep into it.

GARDEN TOAST (A.K.A. PERFECTION)

Pleasure in the job puts perfection in the work.
—ARISTOTLE

I think by now most of us know who Marie Kondo is. Perhaps you've read her runaway bestseller *The Life-Changing Magic of Tidying Up* and are currently gently rolling your socks, which, according to Kondo, is how socks prefer to be stored in drawers. If you don't know who Marie Kondo is, she's a Japanese organizing consultant and author who has sold millions of books, has a show on Netflix (*Tidying Up with Marie Kondo*), and developed the KonMari method, which has seen millions of closets and drawers go from messy to pristine.

Kondo views tidying up not as a chore but as an *event*—something to be enjoyed, handled in small steps and by category (there's an order for how to tidy your house top to bottom, and it's quite precise). KonMari converts are asked to only keep things that spark joy and get rid of items that don't, with a "thank you" to the item as it is banished forever.

Apparently, Kondo has been super into organization her entire life. She says that as a child, she used to run back into the classroom to tidy the bookshelves while her classmates played in physical education class. She also founded her own organization consultancy when she was only 19 years old. When you see her onscreen, she is petite and flawlessly put together, and one can only imagine the state of her home—organized top to bottom, with joy-sparking minimalism the main decor. I have had fantasies of living like that, though if I'm being honest, I own but have not finished the book, and while I *did* organize my clothing drawers and roll my socks, I am many, many junk drawers and closets away from it being life-changing.

In truth, it exhausts me, the idea of striving for such perfection in my home environment. Even though I'm sure I would love it . . . if someone else would do it for me. It also feels impossible, because I do not live alone. I have a husband and a 12-year-old daughter and two guinea pigs and one labradoodle living with me, and more days than not, our lives are busy and messy and our house is *lived in*—which I wish was a compliment, like saying "It's so cozy!" but I know it's not.

Recently Marie Kondo was featured in a profile where she had to admit that her home is not as organized as she would like. She said, "To be honest, my situation has changed since I was single. I've let go of needing to maintain a perfect home all the time." Her "situation" now involves a husband and two children under the age of five, and suddenly Marie Kondo is all of us—longing for perfection, and even having expertise in how to *get* it, but realizing it's not attainable most days. Welcome to the club, Marie.

This seems a good time to let you in on a secret: it's okay to aim for "just fine" or "good enough," even if that gets you nowhere near Marie Kondo–level *perfect*.

My daughter is not the tidiest of sorts. This is not out of character for the tween set, and I have spent a lot of breath asking her to clean up her room. But here's what I've learned: no matter how many times I demonstrate the folding of shirts, pants, *socks*, she does some sort of roll-and-stuff move when she puts her clothes away. One leg of a pair of pants or a shirt arm is usually hanging off the closet shelf, and when I point it out, she'll shrug and say, "Good enough." *And guess what?* She is not wrong. Does it matter if the shirt arm hangs down? No, it does not. In fact, she has argued, it's more efficient because she can pull that shirt off the shelf more easily, by its arm. Good enough.

Time to check in with yourself. Are you in the "good enough" or the "never good enough" camp? When you think about taking that first slice of cake or waking up at 5 a.m. to reclaim some time, are logistical challenges holding you back from committing? Or is it that damn fear roadblock, whispering that you may not be as successful with it as you'd like to be? Whichever it is, I have some great news: it doesn't matter.

Once again, *it doesn't matter*.

This is not to say your project, or perhaps your challenges around it, aren't important. They are—otherwise, we wouldn't be having this conversation about accepting "good enough." But what *doesn't matter* is how you go about it, or how many attempts it takes you to get out of bed after setting that first alarm, or whether you manage to Marie Kondo your time.

I recently saw an Instagram post featuring something called garden toast. It was basically avocado toast, but with a serious artistic flair: the toast was piled high with artfully arranged edible flowers and other garden-procured greens. It was beautiful, and it made me feel sad about my lowly toast that morning, with a half a smashed avocado and a sprinkle of salt and chili pepper. How utterly boring! But this highlights how trying *too hard* has its own set of problems—avocado toast is already delicious, and turning it into something too pretty to eat is not necessarily making it better.

Consider how you want to use your time, particularly in that early-morning window. Avoid the compulsion to create your own version of garden toast or apply KonMari levels of perfection, and instead keep your momentum by focusing on the concept of "good enough."

IT'S NOT DEPRIVATION,
IT'S OPPORTUNITY

The best is yet to be.
—ROBERT BROWNING

f you've ever spent time with someone who does CrossFit, you probably understand a few things:

1. CrossFitters can be obsessive sorts who use a specific language—mainly acronyms—to discuss movements and exercises: WOD (workout of the day), AMRAP (as many rounds as possible), EMOM (every minute on the minute), OT2M (on the two minutes), etc.

2. CrossFit is *intense*, and there is much focus on performance over anything else.

3. It's super-annoying if you don't do CrossFit to spend a lot of time with people who do.

I say all of this with a deep love for and appreciation of CrossFit. When I turned 46, I decided it was time to rediscover my muscles. I've always been active—at times obsessively so—but after a knee injury and two years of rehabilitation, I had . . . softened, both in body and spirit. As someone who enjoys exercise, I was looking for something to really push me. Enter CrossFit, a full-body, high-intensity workout that focuses on functional movement and strength. There are no mirrors in our "box" (the term used for a CrossFit gym), which is basically a converted industrial space. You won't find weight machines or aerobics classes here—all classes are run by a "coach," and while CrossFit can feel more "torture session" than "exercise class," it works: the muscles are coming back, and I feel stronger than I ever have in my life. I also often can't walk up (or down) stairs without wincing after a particularly brutal lunges day, and on occasion trying to brush my hair makes my arms scream in agony. But it's amazing! You should try it! (Refer to point #3 above.)

One other thing CrossFitters are committed to, aside from punishing exercise, is nutrition to help support said punishing exercise. Our gym was running a nutrition challenge that my husband and I decided (without thinking too much about it) to join. The goal was clear: add muscle, lose fat, increase your performance in the gym. Now that I was someone who went from having no clue what a WOD was to owning *two* pairs of cross-training shoes, plus custom-made wrist wraps, gymnastics grips, and a skipping rope (you skip a shit-ton, and no, it isn't fun like it used to be when you were a kid), I felt I was ready to tackle the nutrition challenge. Sure, it meant I couldn't have bread, cheese, bourbon, or sugar—some of my favourite things—but there was the opportunity to increase my energy and strength, and maybe even see my abs again.

In order to survive a month of this, I had to see the opportunities and not the deprivations. Which is exactly how I suggest you look at rising early to do that thing you've always wanted to do but haven't yet been able to squeeze into your daily schedule. *It's not about what you're losing, but what you're gaining.*

Another critical component here is fun and enjoyment. There are many areas of life where you don't have an option, but when it comes to how you choose to spend your 4% fix hour, if it isn't fun—or worse, is making you unhappy— please stop. *Immediately.* As a wise friend of mine said when I was lamenting the sadness of high-protein coconut-flour banana muffins that were like hockey pucks, "Life is not meant to feel like a giant bowl of bran." This goes for nutrition challenges at the gym and early-morning projects alike. If it isn't fun, at least most of the time, or you aren't enjoying the benefits of what you're doing, what the hell is the point of doing it?

Think back to the last time you did something that was supposed to be fun but wasn't. For me, it's ice-skating. Because I live in a climate where there is snow and the ground is frozen for a solid four months of the year, ice-skating is a major pastime. I grew up on a hobby farm, which was quite an idyllic childhood for me and my sister. Not only did we have acres to roam and explore, but we made maple syrup from our trees and hatched chicks and had pet ducks and were raised by hippies who believed in free-range parenting. *Idyllic*. In the winter, my parents would flood part of our lawn for an ice rink, and while it wasn't exactly a professional job—I still remember the feeling of my teeth chattering as my skates bumped over the many imperfections in the ice's surface—it was *fun*.

Fast-forward a bunch of years and I'm a teenager ice-skating at an outdoor rink. The ice is smoother, but there are dozens of others skating at the same time, and so we're all forced to skate in the same oval pattern around the rink. Plus, the skates are more uncomfortable than I remember, and the hot chocolate is watered down. Huh. Less fun this time.

Fast-forward a few more years and I'm a grown-up, skating for the first time in years, in an ice arena. Gone is the feel of cold, crisp outdoor air, the attempts to chase my sister around the rink, the games and the joy of zigzagging across the ice because we could. Again, everyone is skating in a circle . . . and when the buzzer goes, we start skating the other direction. It begins to feel like I am in a traffic jam, but with very uncomfortable footwear and someone else's playlist.

I haven't gone skating since and have announced my retirement from it, even though I have a young daughter who would probably like to go ice-skating with her mother. Despite it being an activity so many people love and think is *super-fun*, it doesn't resonate that way for me.

Without question, getting out of bed earlier than you absolutely have to could feel like deprivation. After all, you are inevitably committing to less slumber, at least until you sort out your sleep schedule so you're off to bed earlier. And as we've discussed, the last thing you need to add to your already-too-high adulting pile is sleep deprivation. It's fair to feel irritated and resistant to the idea of trying out the morning lark lifestyle.

However, behind that wall of things you might need to give up is a glittery pot of opportunities. This is your chance to change your narrative from "I wish I could, but I just don't have the time" to "I decided it was worth it—I was worth it—and somehow found the time!" Opportunity is always within reach, but you need to know what you want and be prepared to shift a few things to make it happen.

As my husband repeatedly tells me when I'm struggling with my writing and declare that perhaps I should change careers to barista or librarian, "If it was easy, everyone would do it."

PART THREE: RESCUE YOUR TIME (FIND, AND USE, THAT LIFE PRESERVER)

Time isn't the main thing. It's the only thing.
—MILES DAVIS

THE CHOICE IS YOURS

For the past 33 years, I have looked in the mirror every morning and asked myself: "If today were the last day of my life, would I want to do what I am about to do today?" And whenever the answer has been "No" for too many days in a row, I know I need to change something.
—STEVE JOBS, 2015 STANFORD UNIVERSITY COMMENCEMENT SPEECH

F ern Resort is only a couple of hours north of Toronto and is somewhat reminiscent in style to the resort in the movie *Dirty Dancing*—but without a Patrick Swayze character or any of the drama. Along with activities like scavenger hunts and water sports and obstacle courses and candy bingo for the kids, they also offer adult camp fun, with axe-throwing and tennis lessons and beer-tasting, to name a few options.

On a recent visit with my husband's family, my sister-in-law and I decided to do the morning yoga. It was exactly as described—stretchy, mindful, lakeside, serene. Until it started to rain. "No problem," Kathy, the instructor, said, "we can move inside." We quickly grabbed our yoga mats and headed indoors, at which point it became clear we weren't the only ones with that idea. A camp group of young boys was also sharing the theatre space, and they were playing Nerf gun tag. If you've never been in the same room as a group of boisterous young boys playing Nerf gun tag, let me tell you, you can barely hear yourself think.

As we settled into the meditation portion of our yoga hour, Kathy looked concerned as she watched the boys playing, and we (all of us parents or grandparents) assured her it would be just fine. If there's one thing parents of young children can do, it's tune out the voices of children who don't belong to them. Onward we went, our yoga group lying eyes-closed on our mats in the semi-darkened room in the shavasana pose, as Kathy recited meditation mantras. Something about an ocean and the waves and I have no clue what else, because I had to tune her out as well as the Nerf gun tag game that was going on around us. An outsider would have laughed at the scene: yogis on one side of the room, an all-out Nerf gun battle happening just feet away. To say those of us on our mats had conflicting priorities would be an understatement. How do you fully relax into a meditation when there is so much noise and intense activity happening nearby? And yet, we managed. Some of us may have even dozed off amidst the cacophony of meditative mantras, Kathy's soft and gentle voice, the sounds of yoga music, and the yells and shouts of boys delightedly shooting Nerf guns.

Our world is full of conflicting priorities, not dissimilar to finding your Zen while a game of Nerf gun war happens ten feet from your yoga mat. We face conflicts between family responsibilities and work responsibilities, between exercise goals and the need for rest and relaxation, between cleaning the house, mowing the lawn, and driving the kids to and from activities. Sometimes you do have to choose, but oftentimes you can address multiple priorities without having to let one go by the wayside.

This is where the previous suggestions of mini-goals and a Focused Four list can be helpful, as both allow you to home in on your priorities—every day, if that's your thing, or at least weekly—to ensure that if you have conflicts (and of course you do), you can find a way past them. It does not have to be an *either/or* situation. It can be a case of *and*, as long as you are clear about what you want to accomplish and realistic about how you're going to do it.

When we look at U.S.-based data on studies measuring happiness from 1956 onwards, we find that while material wealth has increased significantly, levels of happiness remain about the same. Around 30% of people report feeling happy with their lives. Without question, not having the means to reach basic lifestyle levels contributes to unhappiness, but having significantly more resources does not seem to lead to a comparable increase in happiness. All of which tells us something worth zooming in on: it seems that there's more to chase outside of our work and the mighty dollar.

However, if it's our work that keeps us so busy we're unable to find time for ventures that aren't red-line priorities—like, say, writing a novel or making pastry-chef level French macarons or learning to play the piano—then we need to pay even closer attention. If asked about the non-work time we have available each day, many of us would likely report that we have little of it, and that it seems to be shrinking. Even with a host of tools and resources at our disposal that are intended to make life easier than it has ever been (think smartphones and the internet).

If the conflict between being merely satisfied or being happy comes down to one of these red-line priorities, like choosing between work (and quite necessary income) and less work (so, less income), it can be hard to justify the trade. I imagine we all crave more time to ourselves and greater happiness, but we also all have bills to pay. Don't force yourself to choose. You can still find your "om" amidst a roaring game of Nerf gun tag, as long as you're willing to be creative about your time.

WRITE IT DOWN

It takes as much energy to wish as it does to plan.
—ELEANOR ROOSEVELT

As anyone who has spent time at a cottage knows, a too-strong wind or a single lightning bolt can easily take out the power, sometimes for long stretches of time. When this happens at our cottage—and because we never know if the power will be out for five minutes or six days—we trigger the power-outage action plan: the fridge and freezer remain closed, and if you have to get something out, be coordinated and speedy; all cooking happens on the propane barbecue; flashlights and candles come out, as do board and card games; and "mellow yellow" rules apply.

Last summer, when we were visiting the cottage, the power blipped out for about two seconds and came right back—no storm in sight, so we expected it would stay on. My daughter, who was 11 and had spent a lot of time up at the cottage with her grandparents, shouted from the bedroom, "We need to fill buckets and pots with water!" Then she appeared before me, eyes wide and expression purposeful.

"No, we don't," I said. "The power is back on. All good."

"We need to be *prepared*. We always fill up pots when the power goes out. What if we can't get water?"

(Did I mention that the cottage sits on a lake?)

"Then we'll go into town."

Exasperated with me, she said, "What if *they* run out of water?"

While I might need to speak with my parents about inducing water-shortage anxiety in my kid during summer vacations, the blame probably rests a touch closer to home. When I relayed the "fill the pots!" story to a friend, she said, "She is *so* your kid." I like to be prepared, what can I say?

Aside from keeping my phone fully charged and a cupboard full of Lysol wipes during flu season, plus always having granola bars in my car and dental floss in my purse, one of the main ways my preparatory side comes out is through pen-to-paper note-taking. My general mantra goes something like this: *If you want something to happen, write it down.*

There are a couple of oft-quoted studies about the value of writing things down, specifically goals. It's likely you've heard some of the results of these studies—typically referred to as the Yale and Harvard goals studies—or have even used the findings in conversation, or perhaps in a presentation at some point in your school or work life. It was research I certainly leaned heavily on during my management consulting years. While the Yale and Harvard studies were done at different times and looked at slightly different parameters, here's what both studies found: when evaluated years later, students who wrote down their goals were significantly more successful and wealthier than their peers who did *not* log goals. In fact, the Harvard study findings were boiled down to this gem, which has been exploited by many self-help and motivational gurus over the years: only 3% of the MBA students in the study said they wrote down goals; 10 years later, they had accumulated 97% of the wealth of their entire graduating class. So the goal documenters were more successful, according to the results, and this study suggested it had everything to do with writing down their goals.

Could it really be that easy to achieve such success? We merely need to write our goals down? It's such a simple premise that it almost feels too good to be true . . . which is exactly what it turned out to be. The results were fabricated somewhere along the way and—newsflash!—neither the Harvard study nor the Yale study actually happened.

But while the line between writing down goals and achieving success is neither as straight nor as clearly demarcated as these bogus studies suggested, there *is* evidence that writing down your goals isn't a willy-nilly exercise. One study done by Professor Gail Matthews of the Psychology Department at the Dominican University of California offers insight into how we can make goals stick. Matthews found that achieving our goals is, in fact, influenced by writing them down, committing to goal-directed action steps, and then being accountable for those actions. Study participants were divided into five groups, ranging from those who simply thought about their goals (and mentally rated them in terms of difficulty, importance, and achievability) to those who wrote down and rated goals, came up with action steps to achieve them, and shared progress on those steps with a trusted friend via weekly reports. That final group, the one that went so far as to send weekly reports to a friend for accountability, achieved significantly more goals than all the other groups. However, it was determined that the groups that wrote down their goals, versus merely thinking about them, also made significant strides in achieving those objectives. So while it might not lead to the incredible wealth and success percentages touted by the phony Harvard and Yale studies, you *are* more likely to achieve something if you write it down. Pen to paper, brain to hand, abstract to concrete.

Writer Antoine de Saint-Exupéry famously said, "A goal without a plan is simply a wish." Which brings me to my decades-old bucket list. I had clear intentions when I started that list, but as a teenager with limited life experience, the concept of how to work my way through the items—many of which were big and bold—felt vast and blurry. One of the ways I discovered to ensure I checked items off was to share the list with people I trusted, and talk ad nauseam with them about the items on it. Including item #34: *Write a novel*. This was an odd entry at the time (and came in just above *Milk a cow*, which I have yet to check off), because at the age of 17, I had no interest in novel writing, let alone becoming a full-time writer. That wouldn't enter my consciousness for another 20 years. Yet, here I am, a novelist, some 30 years later.

If anything can convince me there's power in writing something down, this is it.

GO WITH THE FLOW

We are what we repeatedly do. Excellence, therefore,
is not an act but a habit.
—WILL DURANT

G ail Vance Civille, the *Red Jell-O, sweet* sensory scientist we met earlier, is self-admittedly frustrating
to share a meal with. Because her taste buds are so
finely trained, it can be hard, if not impossible, for her to
shut that off when she isn't working. She told me how, when
dining at a restaurant with her family, she's been known to
become so focused on the taste and texture of her meal that
she'll close her eyes, ignore everything and everyone around
her, and go full tilt into sensory analysis. Civille essentially
enters a "flow state," much to the annoyance of her children,
she says.

The term "flow state" was popularized by Hungarian-American psychologist Mihaly Csikszentmihalyi, who defined it as "an optimal state of consciousness where we feel our best and perform our best." If you wonder whether you've ever entered such a state before, think about a time when you became so absorbed in an activity that time essentially disappeared. It can happen to me when I listen to audiobooks or podcasts, read, or am "in the zone" with my writing—sometimes two hours will pass when I'm only partially aware of the world around me.

The opposite experience happens when we're trying to multi-task. While some, particularly women, claim to be efficient multi-taskers, studies have not proven we can effectively focus on many tasks at once. And while women *do* seem to perform slightly better than men when they, for example, are required to listen to a story being streamed through earphones while also reading another story on a screen (retaining content as well), humans are not well suited to this sort of multi-focus situation. Our nervous systems can process about 110 bits of information per second, which seems like a lot (and it is). But in order to, for example, listen to a friend telling you a story and then *understand* what's being said, you need to process about 60 bits of information per second. So if a second friend chimes in at the same time to tell her own story, good luck being able to give your focus to both friends' stories and, further, to retain and understand each one equally.

Our ability to process a finite amount of information each second explains why it's hard to listen to two or more voices at once, or to read this sentence and another one simultaneously and capture the content and meaning of both. Simply put, our brains do not have the capacity to multi-task when we need to focus.

When you're in the aforementioned flow state, experiencing a level of intense focus, you don't have enough information-processing energy left over to pay attention to the other cues around you. (Like maybe how your butt is pins and needles from sitting in the chair for so long without changing position, or that you're starving because you missed lunch, or that the dog is whining by the back door, or that a family member or co-worker is trying to ask you a question.) Basically, all your attention is required to focus on the task at hand, and so your existence (and everything else in your world) is temporarily suspended for that block of time.

The mental state of flow involves being entirely involved in an activity for its own sake. Csikszentmihalyi identified 10 conditions necessary to enter such a state:

1. Having clear goals about what you want to achieve.

2. Concentration and focus.

3. Participating in an intrinsically rewarding activity.

4. Losing feelings of self-consciousness.

5. Timelessness; losing track of time passing.

6. Being able to immediately judge your own progress; instant feedback on your performance.

7. Knowing that your skills align with the goals of the task.

8. Feeling control over the situation and the outcome.

9. Lack of awareness of physical needs.

10. Complete focus on the activity itself.

Now, according to Csikszentmihalyi, when it comes to creativity and getting into a flow, you don't experience this sort of suspension from existence without some practice—even if you can check off each of the above conditions. When he studied musicians, scientists, novelists, and other creators able to tap into this suspended experience, he found they had at least 10 years of practice in their field—which is more than you currently have when it comes to a new 4% fix experience.

However, that doesn't mean you can't enter a Zen-like focused state for this experience, even if it's the first time you're attempting it. We know our ability to process information—and comprehend and retain it—is reliant on being focused on a single task. We also know that distractions that force us to multi-task are counterproductive to entering this state of suspension. So, knowing all of this, we can set up a scenario that caters to our needs and offers a "best case" environment—like one that is free of distractions.

When I'm drafting a novel, one of the best ways for me to ensure a "pat on the back" writing session is to head to a coffee shop. You might think it would be an incredibly distracting environment, and it definitely can be, especially when early-morning running groups arrive for their post-run caffeine hit. However, what I've learned is that if I bring earbuds and play the same set of one to five songs on repeat while I write, I can spend hours in the coffee shop, with dozens of people coming and going and constant activity around me, without really breaking stride. Essentially, the familiar, consistent playlist means my brain isn't working to continually process the songs and their lyrics. Also, being able to glance up and see people moving about—without being required to *pay attention* to their conversations—gives me tiny moments of distraction that don't push me off track but are effective in reducing my procrastination impulses.

Now, it's all fine and good to talk about removing distractions and setting up a "go with the flow" environment that allows you to find the focus you need. However, this can be a really tough thing to do, even if you have very few barriers to your time. Because ultimately, we all have running to-do lists, and in my case, if I don't get them down on paper and organized, the list items run through my brain on a near-constant loop . . . and they are especially shouty when I'm trying to focus.

Here's how I manage my to-dos so I'm not multi-tasking in this way. I take a piece of paper and draw two vertical lines, so I have three evenly spaced columns. At the top of the first column, I write *To Do*; in the second, I write *Must Do*; and in the third, I write *For Later* (or *Put a Goddamn Pin in It*, depending on my mood). Then I take a few moments and write down everything under *To Do* that is weighing me down or is outstanding. Finally, I start moving stuff around. The *Must Do* column is exactly as it sounds: the task must be done (like, it's a 24- to 48-hour priority), and by me. The *For Later* column is for everything that can either wait at least 48 hours or be handled by someone else (be sure to put a name beside the item in this case, and let that person know, because no one is a mind reader). I make these sorts of lists every few days, or at a minimum once a week. And if an item that is a *Must Do* is still on the list at week's end, I line up the jelly beans or chocolate chips as rewards for my willpower and get to it.

DON'T BE FUSSY

The way I see it, if you want the rainbow,
you gotta put up with the rain.
—DOLLY PARTON

'm not sure exactly how I agreed to drive my daughter 45 minutes—each way—to a horse-riding camp a few towns over for one week each summer, but while my back and my work productivity suffer during that week, there is also a silver lining to this drive: a little bakery in the middle of nowhere, directly on our route. This bakery is run by one of the most no-nonsense women I have ever met, and though our interactions have been brief, I remain both terrified and in awe of her gruffness—counter to the happiness her melt-in-your-mouth pastries induce.

You can never be sure exactly when this bakery will be open, and once the daily baked goods run out, that's it, you're out of luck, no matter how badly you're craving an apple cider doughnut. The owner can be crustier than the outside of the delicious breads she bakes, but it's all worth it because her butter tarts are mind-blowing, as are her pickles, jams, pies, quiches, muffins . . . you get the idea. She may not always be cheery, but her creations are worth every scowl.

On one particular visit she was uncharacteristically chatty and was lamenting a call she had taken just before I arrived—from a woman who wanted to buy a pie. She told me this woman had a lot of pie questions but mostly wanted to know when the bakery would have fresh blackberry pie, and she was quite insistent it *had* to be blackberry.

"Blackberry pie? Who wants blackberry pie?" the owner grumbled as she packed up my strawberry-rhubarb pies. "So, you know what I did?" I shook my head and stayed quiet, grateful that blackberries are my least favourite fruit so I would never be requesting such a pie.

"I hung up," she said. "Just hung right up. No one wants blackberry pie. No one."

Wisely, I didn't offer the observation that clearly *this* woman she had just hung up on wanted a blackberry pie, because I was happy to have my hands full of my own, far superior fruit pies. I suspected said woman would not be paying the bakery a visit in the future, nor would the owner of said bakery ever be making a blackberry pie. Fussiness over pie would not be tolerated.

I was editing this book during the early days of the COVID-19 pandemic, which was a time when there was little room for fussiness to flourish. As with the bakery, where "you get what you get and you don't get upset," things we used to take for granted—like choosing the precise brand and style of toilet paper or scent of disinfecting wipes, or finding a shelf teeming with bread yeast and a variety of flours—were no longer an option. If you managed to score a package of toilet paper, it was worthy of multiple social media posts, and who cared how many plies it had or whether it was quilted? Also, snagging a grocery order pickup or delivery slot became somewhat of a sport, and even if you could get a slot, the contents of the order were often a surprise. I'm a vegetarian, and firm tofu is a staple of my diet. However, because people were stocking up on non-meat items, it was hard to get. So when silken tofu, which is basically the consistency of thick yogurt, was subbed for my usual firm variety, I cheerily said, "Oh, it's fine! I'll just make something *soft!*" My daughter gave me a concerned look, but we later discovered that silken tofu actually works really well in banana bread.

Subscribing to the idea of needing things to be *just so* (a.k.a. fussiness) as the only way to stimulate action can be a time trap. We may then find ourselves in a continuous, unproductive loop: being rigid with our expectations, and then feeling disappointed when reality doesn't match up. This also applies when thinking about how you want to use your early-morning energy. If you're too persnickety about your 4% fix endeavour, you're upping the chances you'll never start it in the first place. Or, you'll spend that hour doing the equivalent of taking a step forward, then another step back, and never making progress.

Being fussy with that first hour can show up a lot of different ways: deciding that if you snooze through your alarm, it's not really worth the hassle of getting up because you've already lost 15 minutes; putting so many conditions on your endeavour, it's like trying to put IKEA furniture together without instructions or an Allen key; retooling your potential 4% fix list over and over, perhaps adding it to a bullet journal and spending the whole time decorating the page; writing endless to-do lists that are really just busywork; or committing to getting up early *only* when conditions *x*, *y*, and *z* are met, and your kids have finally learned to turn lights off when they leave the room and Mercury is no longer in retrograde.

This is a long list, but it is not exhaustive. However, it shows how easy it is to come up with reasons why something *can't* work versus seeking out the "how" to make it happen.

It's important to note that fussiness is not the same thing as thoughtfulness. You should be as clear as you can about the *what* and the *why* of your venture, taking into consideration both your ikigai and what's worth getting out of bed for. *Knowing* what you want—unless it comes to blackberry pie at that out-of-town bakery—is critical to ensure you *get what you want* out of that first hour. But if you were counting on all-purpose flour and something called kamut flour ends up in your grocery bag instead, find a new recipe and pivot.

A LITTLE GOES A LONG WAY

A little progress each day adds up to big results.
—SATYA NANI

I n Malcolm Gladwell's 2008 book, *Outliers*, the world was reminded of the "practice makes perfect" concept in a very specific way, via Gladwell's "10,000-hour rule," which states that it takes approximately that many hours of practising something to become a genius at it. He wrote that 10,000 hours is "the magic number of greatness" and offered examples of this in history, from Bill Gates to the Beatles to concert violinists. Gladwell posited that science could in fact give us a number for how long it takes to develop expertise, and that became the foundation for this rule, and for *Outliers*.

But here's the thing: 10,000 hours is a long damn time. It's 416 days, if you could use all 24 hours each and every day. And if you only had one hour to dedicate to something daily . . . well, we can all do the math. We're looking at 10,000 days. Or 27 years. So, if I start trying to become a skilled macaron baker—a personal goal of mine—this year, by Gladwell's rule I should be a grand macaron master by the time I'm 74. Huh.

Naturally, there have been critics of this 10,000-hour rule. And in the years since the book was published, Gladwell's rule has been challenged and, some would argue, debunked. Josh Kaufman, the author of *The First 20 Hours: How to Learn Anything . . . Fast*, completely dismisses Gladwell's 10,000-hour rule as a myth. Rather, Kaufman figures that if you dedicate a mere 20 hours to the practice of something (about 45 minutes a day, for a month), you can learn a new skill. Granted, it seems Malcolm Gladwell was thinking bigger than simply acquiring a new skill; he was focused on becoming brilliant in a certain field.

But Kaufman's stance is certainly more palatable to those of us who want to branch out and embark on something new but are overwhelmed by (or frankly, not interested in) the idea of investing 10,000 hours into it. Because, let's be honest, do I really want to bake macarons every day for 27 years? No, I do not. I don't need to be a genius or an expert to be "good enough" at making these beloved French confections. I simply want to learn how to make a recipe consistently well, so that I can pull it out once or twice a year to impress my mother-in-law or my daughter's friends.

If we opt in to the "a little goes a long way" concept, it's conceivable that with a moderate amount of dedication and focus—let's even bump Kaufman's 45 minutes to one hour a day—we could be well on our way to learning one new skill per month, and a dozen per year. Now, learning a dozen skills or tackling a similar number of wish list projects a year may be excessive—and might even take us into BHAG territory, which, as previously discussed, we would be wise to avoid.

When I first started running long distance, I was in that spot of being highly committed but inappropriately skilled. The bulk of my experience to that point had involved jogs with my dad when I was kid, which I did mostly for the pre-run spoonful of honey he always doled out. But on my bucket list was *Complete a half marathon*, and so even though the thought of running for two hours felt impossible, I wanted to give it a try.

Before I set out on my first training run, I made a rule for myself: I only had to run for 10 minutes. If it was still awful at that point, I was allowed to stop. But I knew if I could make it through that first bit, I would likely keep going. During the four months I trained, I think I stopped at 10 minutes twice. By the time I ran the half marathon, I could run for 2 hours without stopping. All because I started with a small, manageable 10-minute rule and built from there.

That wasn't the first time I recognized the value of compounded experience. By the time my first book was published, my second one was already in the final stages of copy-editing with my publisher. People often asked what I was working on next—assuming I was dabbling in an early draft of book two—and I told them I was halfway into my third novel. There was often a pause, then a questioning look. "But . . . isn't this your *first* book?" Though it seemed like I was extraordinarily prolific, it was much less impressive than that. Because if you write 500 words a day for 160 days, you will end up with an 80,000-word manuscript. That's a full-length novel completed in just under 6 months of work. Now, a large chunk of those words may—likely will—suck. There's a good chance you'll have to spend many more months editing said novel or writing project, because we all do. But—and this is not to be taken lightly—at 80,000 words you have a solid "No shit, I did it" first draft.

If writing is not your thing, no worries. The basic principle applies regardless: you need less time than you think, and you *can* find the time you need.

When it comes to a 4% fix hour, try making a similar 10-minute rule for yourself. Even if that's your limit, giving yourself those 10 minutes per day (minutes that previously belonged to something or someone else) will mean you've uncovered 5 extra hours a month you didn't realize you had. Sure, that won't get you to Malcolm Gladwell levels of mastery, but that's *60 hours a year* you can now dedicate to something you never imagined you'd have time for.

DROP A BALL OR TWO

It is not enough to be busy; so are the ants.
The question is: What are we busy about?
—HENRY DAVID THOREAU

work from home and find it a challenge to focus on work tasks when, say, my kitchen is a mess. Or the dog is giving me the eyes to go for a walk. Or I think I could get a few loads of laundry done in between editing my chapters. All these mini-distractions can cannibalize my work time, and sometimes I end up going to the library or a coffee shop just so the laundry hamper doesn't call my name and the guilt about the dog is temporarily removed.

Inevitably you have set up your life to have very little free time most days. Whether your time is occupied by work, kids, pets, aging parents, volunteering, or making sure there's food in the refrigerator so you don't have to order takeout *yet again*, my guess is that most of your day is quite full, perhaps down to the minute. Which leaves little time to consider tackling something that isn't viewed as "mandatory." And yet that's precisely why you should consider doing something that isn't viewed as mandatory! Rescuing your time begins by acknowledging you don't have enough of it, and then sorting out what's keeping you so busy and deciding if you can let go of any of it without the wheels falling off the bus. It's the nirvana of modern time management—being able to check off your to-dos and still find some R&R in each day.

There's this newfangled thing where we wear "I'm so busy!" or "I'm exhausted; I only slept *x* hours last night" badges with honour. Which really is pretty dumb of us, right? Since when did being so busy become a *good* thing? Why do we talk about how little we sleep in a competitive tone? ("Well, I would have killed for your 6 hours! I only got 4.") Trying to do all the things every day is unrealistic—we know this, because we have years of practice. Yet, somehow, many of us, based on our terrifyingly complex schedules, continue to hold on to the belief it *is* possible.

It is not. It never has been. We are not much different from our parents and grandparents; in fact, studies show we have *more* free time than previous generations, thanks to modern conveniences such as dishwashers and laundry machines and microwaves. Except we also have technology, like hand-held devices that are *supposed* to make our lives easier but instead allow us to work and make schedules from anywhere, anytime. Perhaps one of the most depressing examples of being shackled to busyness that I ever read came from a 2012 *Atlantic* article by Anne-Marie Slaughter titled "Why Women Still Can't Have It All." In it, Slaughter talked about a mom who keyed 2:22 or 1:11 or 3:33 into her microwave timer because pressing only one number saved her time. When we're strategizing how to maximize our efficiency when setting our microwave timers, I think it's safe to say we're in need of a "busyness" intervention.

Like a lot of us, Brigid Schulte wears many hats, every day. Not only is she a mom of busy kids, she's also a journalist at the *Washington Post*, a *New York Times* bestselling author, and the director of the *Better Life Lab* podcast. If anyone can claim (over)busyness, it's Brigid Schulte. When I spoke with her, she was just coming off delivering back-to-back keynote addresses, as well as keeping up with her regular day-to-day activities, and she was tired. Schulte is quick to say that while she has interviewed pretty much every time expert out there, has written a bestseller on the issue, and frequently talks about the subject to large audiences, she herself remains a "work in progress." She talks about our tendencies to "overwork and overparent and overdo," and in her book, *Overwhelmed: Work, Love, and Play When No One Has the Time*, she discusses how we have lost the plot when it comes to our leisure time. As a result, so many of us are under extreme pressure and stress, which leads to a variety of very bad things, including chronic illness.

The deep dive into exploring leisure came after the late sociologist Dr. John Robinson (dubbed "Father Time" by his colleagues) suggested to Schulte that her time diary showed she had 27 hours of (untapped) leisure time a week. This came as a huge surprise to Schulte, who felt she had next to no leisure time. However, she soon realized what

Dr. Robinson was calling "leisure time" was in fact nothing of the sort. He was collecting the 5- and 10-minute "in between time" breaks throughout Schulte's day (time that was, say, between dropping one kid off at a sporting activity and having to go pick up the other one) and adding it up as "leisure time." True, those mini-chunks weren't spoken for, but they also weren't useful, or enjoyable, blocks of time.

"For you to have the full experience of leisure . . . and what is that?" Schulte says. "Not work time? Not childcare time? Leisure is its own category, not the absence of work or 'drudge' work." It requires two active things, she adds: that you have *freely chosen* what you're filling that time with, and that you have *control* over the time. Ten minutes on a cold bench at the ice rink, while not specifically fitting into a category like "work" or "childcare" or "housework" (categories Robinson used when analyzing time diaries), is not exactly leisure time, either.

"Women's time, in particular and over history, is so fragmented, and they find it difficult to feel that they've earned leisure time," Schulte says, explaining the guilt we often feel about taking these "non-productive" breaks. What do we do when we're always being pulled away by a million distractions? How do we get over our guilt and view time for ourselves as necessary as, say, making sure the kids have healthy lunch boxes or an important work deadline is met?

Schulte has a suggestion for how to manage this "drop a ball or two" idea of mine, and how to figure out where the fun and joy and leisure can fit into your packed-to-the-rafters schedule: *you have to schedule in leisure time the way you would any other to-do item on a list.* And once you've scheduled it in and are reliably checking it off that to-do list, then you have created a habit. What do we know about habits? They stick if you keep reinforcing them. So the more you find time in your day for leisure activities, the less strictness you'll need to use when scheduling them in.

Prioritize what matters, not just today but in the future. Which balls can you drop? What's a way to find more time simply by giving up something that isn't rocking your world?

For Schulte, one of the most valuable pieces of advice she learned during her research was this: sometimes you have to act yourself into a new way of thinking, which is easier than thinking your way into a new way of acting. Which is why setting that 5 a.m. alarm and dragging yourself out of bed (at least for the first few mornings) may be what's required to shake things up. We can overthink anything, perhaps forever, but without taking action, we aren't really making a change.

PROCRASTINATION VS. MOTIVATION

The best time to plant a tree was 20 years ago.
The second best time is now.
—CHINESE PROVERB

W riting a book is a lot like rearing a child. There is no definitive "how to" manual, you often feel as though you're doing it all wrong, there are typically five mistakes for every one thing you get right, self-doubt is as predictable as the sunrise, and there is a fantastic sense of accomplishment as you watch your child—or book—grow into something wonderful. And, much like in parenting, there are inevitably points in the journey when you find yourself at a crossroads and need to call in reinforcements.

"Why is this book not listening to me?" I bemoaned to two good friends, also novelists. "I'm doing everything right. I'm giving it time and space. I'm putting in the work. I have a great outline. I'm 'listening' . . . *but it won't listen to me.*" As an aside, writers—in case you don't know any personally—are often quite committed to this idea that our books and characters "speak" to us.

These writer friends let me carry on for quite some time. We have a lengthy text thread to prove just how long, actually. There were many excellent suggestions, but ultimately one comment rose to the top.

"You know," one of my friends said, "you're the 'real talk' type, and bullshit isn't your thing. This book needs 'real talk,' *but* it also needs some inspirational 'razzle-dazzle' . . . so maybe that's why it's not listening to you? You're forgetting about the razzle-dazzle?" A legitimate light-bulb moment ensued.

I understand the value of razzle-dazzle—even as a no-nonsense, somewhat anti-inspirational-quote type of person. I get why folks fervently whisper affirmations when they need a boost, and put up posters on office walls, and wear mantra-inscribed T-shirts, and write in notebooks labelled with confidence-boosting messages. I own a desk calendar with wisdoms from Jen Sincero of *You Are a Badass* fame.

Beyond my desk calendar, I also have an extensive collection of mugs that say things like "Nevertheless, She Persisted" and "Seize the Day" and "Not All Who Wander Are Lost," so it's not as though I don't dabble in my own brand of getting revved up and motivated for the task at hand. It is possible, however, to get too hung up on inspiration and razzle-dazzle, which can then lead to you falling short on action. While I find my LET'S DO THIS mug rousing (it's the all caps, I think), if I don't follow through with action and, well, *do the thing*, then my motivation is a lot like filling a balloon with helium and forgetting to tie a knot. *Whoosh*.

Motivation and procrastination are intrinsically linked—if you're feeling unmotivated, you're more likely to procrastinate. And if you procrastinate, it's safe to say your motivation is taking a nap. They are symbiotic, which also means there exists between them a great push and pull. Googling "motivation" brings up a billion-plus hits (plenty of opportunity to procrastinate here). Do the same with the search for "How to stop procrastinating," and you'll have enough material to keep you busy for weeks, which is fantastic news if you're highly motivated to learn more about procrastination. See what I mean?

Procrastination is universal, and we all do it to some degree. Newton's first law of motion states that an object at rest will remain at rest, and if we view procrastination as a "rest" from a must-do task, the task (like the object) will remain at rest and incomplete. The good news is, the other half of the first law of motion states that an object in motion remains in motion, as long as nothing is done to stop it (hello, adorable YouTube animal videos). If you can find a way to push through the procrastination and get to it, chances are you're going to enjoy some much-appreciated momentum.

It might be easy to see how procrastination plays into your day-to-day life. In my case, it often involves an *urgent*, emergency-level need for banana bread baking or a pantry cleanout. In fact, I'm so predictable that now I tell my husband, "If you see me tidying the Lazy Susan, tell me to get back to work, *no matter how hard I try to convince you this must happen now.*" For what it's worth, Lazy Susans can remain cluttered for an eternity, and fresh-baked banana bread is far from essential.

Let me show you how procrastination is screwing you over, particularly with your motivation. Without you even realizing it, every time you say "I wish I could, *but . . .*" you are procrastinating. It's the "but" that's really holding you back—it's what's keeping your "object at rest," and it will remain that way unless you do something about it.

Now, not all procrastination is the same. There's *active* procrastination and *passive* procrastination, and the main difference is this: passive procrastinators are more or less putting things off, but not for long; active procrastinators are essentially ignoring the task, maybe hoping it will simply go away eventually.

In my last novel, I had a problem with one of my main characters, and I didn't know how to solve it. I did what any good author does: I opened my web browser and burrowed in deep. It started with me searching for wartime meals—think one-pan chocolate cake, with no dairy or eggs (it's actually delicious)—and 1950s recipes, which consisted primarily of jellied salads (not as delicious). Somewhere between the chocolate cake and the tuna and lemon jellied salad, I fell into this peanut butter and pickle sandwich rabbit hole, and spent literally *hours* reading about these retro sandwiches. I convinced myself I would work this peanut butter and pickle sandwich into the novel somehow—justification for the hours I spent online—but

I never could find a spot to fit it in. In the meantime, my character was still facing her dilemma and I was no closer to solving the problem.

By comparison, here's how I could have passively procrastinated on the issue: I could have decided to shut my laptop down and go for a walk. To take an hour, or even the rest of the day, to not think about it a moment longer. Then I'd commit to getting up a half hour earlier the next morning to focus solely on that particular problem—doing nothing else until it was solved.

While procrastination is obvious (we're either doing the task that needs to be done, or we're in our second hour of YouTube videos), motivation is a tougher nut to crack. Motivation tends to peak exactly when we don't need it. Say, at 10 p.m. as you're getting into bed and setting that morning alarm, feeling quite certain and confident that *all the things* will happen and go beautifully the next day. But then it's suddenly 6 a.m. and you didn't sleep well and it feels far too early to have your eyes open, let alone get your gym clothes on and be out the door in fifteen minutes. This is exactly when you need motivation to peak and yet . . . *poof*. It disappeared while you slept.

Even those of us who have made a habit of getting up and getting to it require help to ease the battle between motivation and procrastination. For example, I set the coffee maker the night before so all I have to do is push the button when I wake up. I also prepare what I need to focus on the next day ahead of time. This looks either like an actual "call to action" note or list in my manuscript or project, or like a prompt (for example, *Write a character sketch for Lucy, including favourite foods and hobbies and languages she speaks*). Either way, my goal is to prevent my procrastination from bullying my motivation when I sit down for my early-morning 4% fix, and taking a few steps the night before helps me stay on task. Essentially, I've taken the previous day's motivation and paid it forward.

OPERATION PROJECT NAKED

It always seems impossible until it's done.
—NELSON MANDELA

There was a study of 49 German psychology students in which they were asked to fill out a questionnaire on their intentions in choosing psychology as a career. When a student's questionnaire was read out loud (essentially communicating the student's intentions for achieving their goal), the study found the student was less likely to follow through on the behaviours required to achieve that goal. The students whose questionnaires and intentions were *not* read aloud seemed to be more on track with their goal-reaching behaviours, which led to article titles such as "Research Reveals You Should Keep Goals to Yourself" and the more ominous "Why Telling People Your Goals Is a Fatal Mistake." It seemed keeping mum about your goals was the best way to make sure they happened. Stay with me on this, because its relevance will be clear soon enough.

I had not yet read about this study a few years ago, when I was still actively pitching story ideas to magazines. I occasionally spent my 5 a.m. writing sessions brainstorming ideas for magazine pieces, and this particular morning I felt I had come up with a winner. I pitched visiting a nearby nudist resort—where I would take all my clothes off for the day—to see if being naked in public, with other naked people, actually helps you feel better about your body. Women's magazines are full of body confidence pieces and angles, and this was one I hadn't seen before. I was 95% sure the editor would like the idea and so excitedly hit Send and then finished my coffee while I focused on another few story ideas.

Now, as previously mentioned in one of the chapters on sleep, it takes about 25 minutes for caffeine to circulate through your bloodstream. Which meant I had sent the idea to the editor *ahead* of benefitting from the mind-clearing dose of caffeine. Basically, I was half asleep when I sent the pitch. And about 15 minutes later I got a response from the editor. She loved it. Which is when I looked at my 5 a.m. writing companion, my dog, and said, "Oh, shit."

This was the beginning of Operation Project Naked. (In retrospect, I could have been more creative with the project name.) I had eight months to figure out how to get comfortable with the idea of walking around in the nude for the day with complete strangers. One could argue that being naked is the most natural of states and so what's the big deal? Plus, I had grown up with hippie parents who were very comfortable with nudity. Not to mention, I was in my early forties and so old enough to have gained some acceptance for my body. But . . . *but*. A whole day spent naked with similarly disrobed strangers?

Sure, I could have bailed. However, that's not my modus operandi, and besides, what if I learned something amazing through writing the piece? What if I truly felt liberated by spending the day naked? Over the next few months, I told pretty much everyone about my upcoming nudist adventure. I sought out opinions about, um, *grooming,* and whether I should join an extreme exercise class to tighten things up. I forced myself—and my husband—to eat dinner in the nude one night. It was very strange, and I spent most of the meal worrying about a neighbour stopping by to borrow a cup of sugar. But I believed if I talked about it and pushed out of my comfort zone with preparatory things like naked dinners at home, it would be a hell of a lot easier to follow through when it wasn't a dress rehearsal. My goal was to be fully present in the experience, and then to write a kick-ass article about it— and I knew that if I didn't talk about it, I was accountable to only my editor and myself. It's easier to bail on something challenging when you're the only one waiting to see the result.

I do understand why people don't talk about their endeavours, at least before they're sure they're going to work out. Feeling the sting of failure is bad enough without having other people asking you about how things are going, or what went wrong. And when I think about the German study, I can see how *not* sharing your goals could provide the opportunity to see them through—there can be undue pressure to achieve from well-meaning friends, family, and co-workers. However, my personal experience is that people want to help you achieve your goals and are invested in your success in a lovely way because they care about you. Sometimes that's exactly what you need to push past your desire to quit.

While I personally believe a study of only 49 psychology students should not dictate how the rest of us approach goal-setting, I do think how we talk about our goals matters. The fatal mistake is, perhaps, telling people about your goal before you're ready to follow through. Essentially, talking about doing something big, maybe BHAG-level stuff (like writing a first novel), is fun, and you get a rush of excitement when people respond with statements like "Wow, good for you. I can't wait to read it!" Then you go away and sit in front of your laptop with nothing more than an elevator pitch for your story idea and wonder exactly *how* you're going to write the damn thing. Which leads to feelings of insecurity, doubt, and regret, to name a few. Because now you feel you *have* to do it, or you'll be one of those talkers who is not a doer, and you don't want to be *that* person. You dread your friends asking about how the book is going, because four months later you still haven't written anything and it seems the goal is going to remain unrealized in the end. Basically, you feel you've failed before you've even started, and that's a terrible place to hang out.

This is not the ideal scenario in which to find yourself, but it doesn't have to happen like that. Before you start sharing your goals, big or small, you need to be prepared (see the "Write It Down" chapter for a refresher). Do some upfront work, find your footing with the idea, and then plan out a path for its success. Then, when you have a strategy that goes beyond "It's a story about a woman, a dark secret, and the buried treasure that changes everyone's lives," share it with people in your circle who you know will be both positive and supportive, and get to it.

If you're not ready to share your goal with friends and family, seek out groups of similarly minded folks with whom you can share encouraging thoughts and supportive memes. I am part of a morning crew of writers on Twitter who share tweets and support via the #5amwritersclub hashtag, and it has become a necessary part of my goal-achievement strategy when it comes to my writing.

NO, THANKS

The oldest, shortest words—"yes" and "no"—are those which require the most thought.
—Pythagoras

Sometime in the fall of 2019 a meme started floating around social media channels that essentially shared this race-against-time message: *There are only three months left, not only in this year but in this decade, so stop wasting time and start doing all the things you said you were going to do.*

While I'm a fan of setting goals and going after them, this particular message ticked me off. I did not appreciate its tone, and while it might have been motivating for those who shared it, I personally found it affronting. I feel the same way when I see a post that states *You only have x number of summers left with your kids*, which is a great way to ramp that parenting guilt *right up*. PS: You will have many more wonderful experiences with your kids, even beyond summer breaks.

The thing is, your goals do not expire. This should *never* be a race. With a race there are winners and losers, and while a "trophies for all!" mentality comes with its own set of issues, not achieving everything you wanted in a short and specific timeframe in no way means you've failed. There is nothing magical about a new year, nor a new decade. This is taking "new year, new you" to a jacked-up level, and therefore the distance to fall is far greater, the disappointments sharper. So when I saw that meme, I scowled, snort-laughed my disdain, and then said (out loud and to the dog, who was the only one home), "No, *thank you*."

I believe learning to cook five recipes and changing a tire and starting a campfire are all valuable and necessary skills. But learning to use the word "no" more liberally is one of the most useful skills one can adopt. Some may feel that saying yes to all opportunities and requests is not only smart (who knows what might happen as a result?), but also the right thing to do. If someone thinks enough of you to ask, don't you owe them the courtesy of following through on that request? No, you don't.

When I was in my final year of journalism school, and still single, I wrote an article for my magazine class about speed dating. It was before dating went digital, and speed-dating events were popping up everywhere because it was the hot new way to date. As part of my dedication to my research, I decided I would say yes to all blind dates sent my way by well-meaning friends and colleagues. I went on over a dozen blind dates, and I'm here to say . . . sometimes the smartest thing you can do is to say no.

Who remembers Gobstoppers (also known as Jawbreakers)—those rainbow-coloured, multi-layer candy balls that lasted an eternity, each layer a new flavour, and which you had to suck and suck and suck until you got through to the tiny candy ball at its centre? Try to think of your schedule this way: the centre candy ball is your first-hour 4% plan, where your oxygen mask is stored. Those layers surrounding it? *Everything else.* All your "yes" commitments layered upon one another, some of which, on second thought, you wish you had opted out on.

Now, for those of us who grew up eating Gobstoppers, we know if you try to crack right through quickly to get to their more yielding centre, you are risking a high probability of expensive dental work. Similarly, there is no way to just chomp straight through all the layers of distractions and overstuffed schedules and regrettable yesses to get to that oxygen mask, first slice of cake, or 4% fix hour.

Naturally, there will always be things you can't say no to. For everything else, you need to go layer by layer, making choices, getting rid of stuff, asking for help, deciding to do things differently next time, learning to get more comfortable with the highly valuable word "no." One small shift could be to turn off some of the social media notifications on your phone, because engaging with every blip and beep and trill is the equivalent of garden-hosing "Yes, you bet!" responses, in that they erode your focus and screw with your priorities.

Part of the solution to not cracking a tooth on that Jawbreaker of a day in front of you is to let go of this idea that you're letting someone down if you deny the request. This is not easy, but it is necessary if you're going to rescue your time. It helps me to realize that I am not alone in my desire to say yes to more things that *matter to me most*—we are all looking to streamline, because no one has an infinite amount of energy. If I don't decline more often, when I can, I'm actually letting *myself* down.

By opting out of a new engagement or request for your time, what you're really doing is recommitting to the schedule you already have in front of you. One suggestion in Brigid Schulte's aforementioned *Better Life Lab* podcast entitled "Why You're Addicted to Being Busy" was to imagine your week and picture that the thing you're debating saying yes to right now *must* fit into this already hectic week you've scheduled. And if all things considered, you still want to commit, it probably means this activity is important (or exciting or interesting) enough that it deserves a slot. If you can't imagine trying to squeeze it in or having to cancel other commitments to make it work, decline and move on.

You could also embrace one of my favourite methods, which is to imagine how you'll feel if later the event or engagement you're considering agreeing to ends up getting cancelled. If envisioning this scenario results in grand feelings of JOMO (Joy of Missing Out)—a concept reportedly coined in 2012 by tech entrepreneur Anil Dash, and the polar opposite of FOMO (Fear of Missing Out)—it's time to practise your "No, thank you" skills.

TIME TO DIG DEEP

It is easier to resist at the beginning than at the end.
—LEONARDO DA VINCI

I n her TEDx Talk "How to Stop Screwing Yourself Over," author, CNN commentator, and motivational speaker Mel Robbins talks about how to tackle your wake-up. Basically, you are not to linger in bed for a moment longer than necessary once your alarm goes off. No hitting snooze, no checking your phone while still horizontal, no dilly-dallying whatsoever. For Robbins, the only way to "stop screwing yourself over" is to immediately jump out of bed when you hear that alarm. Like, throw off the covers and leap into your day.

I appreciate her approach. I, too, believe hitting snooze is a very bad idea, as all you're doing is temporarily delaying the discomfort of the wake-up. It's not like those few minutes are going to significantly improve your mood or day. If you're arguing with me right now, fine, it's your energy to waste . . . because in your heart of hearts you know this is the truth. Hitting snooze is the equivalent of getting your toddler completely outfitted head to toe in winter gear and then having them proclaim "I have to pee!" You are essentially undoing that moment of readiness—you're taking off the snowsuit, boots, gloves, scarf, hat—every time you hit snooze. And while it might seem like a good idea in the moment—even *necessary*, you might feel—it generally doesn't help anything in the long run. Maybe you gained another 30 minutes in bed by pressing snooze three times, but you also lost the benefit of any real, undisturbed sleep and frittered away half of what could have been an hour to dig into a 4% fix project.

While I agree with Robbins that hitting snooze is a version of "screwing yourself over" and suggest you pretend the snooze button doesn't even exist, I do believe you need a minute longer in the horizontal position to remind yourself why you set the alarm in the first place. It will be tempting to rest in the lull between alarms, but resist . . . there was a reason you decided to do this. So take that one minute or so to mentally engage with why you're getting up—and what's exciting for you about that—and then throw off the covers and leap (or gently roll, as is more likely the scenario) out of bed.

This moment is the beginning of all the great stuff to come, but it's also when the toiling (a.k.a. work) begins.

And yes, even if you've chosen to perfect the baking of French macarons or knit a scarf, or learn to play the piano or master Spanish, it should be handled with the same focus and determination you would give to a critically important job *someone else* has asked you to do. Thanks to the experience of "adulting," we are primed to know what to do with a task we view as work: we get that box checked off, because no one else is going to complete said task on our behalf. So we strategize for its completion by putting in the time and effort.

I've said it before, and this remains true: this first hour, your 4% fix time, is not to be used for work or productivity in the traditional sense. No clearing out of inboxes or creating spreadsheets or planning elaborate strategies. But let's use what we know about how to tackle a work-related project to our benefit and reframe how we approach that early-morning, first-slice-of-cake time.

Dr. Cal Newport, a Georgetown University computer science professor and author, talks about something he terms "deep work," which is when we focus persistently and without distraction (like, from social media and email) on a cognitively demanding yet valuable task. The way we create space for this deep work, Newport says, is by purposefully blocking out chunks of distraction-free time, using a strategy that's called "time blocking."

Keep in mind that, even if you've applied the idea of time blocking to achieve deep work on a project, it doesn't mean you'll actually *achieve* the goal. For example, let's take my 5 a.m. writing time. My goal is to spend at least one hour each morning writing creatively and doing nothing else during that time. But while I am excited and motivated by my writing projects, I also enjoy lazy mornings with a magazine and a pot of coffee. So many 5 a.m. sessions start with me setting up strategies to keep my distraction-seeking brain from procrastinating. One of the most effective things I can do is to eliminate internet surfing when I'm writing. And if my family is up and about and I'm struggling to concentrate, I'll put earbuds in with music that can quickly become white noise (mostly ballads or classical music). These tricks allow me to get into my deep work so that, at the end of my writing session, I'm left with a sense of productivity and positivity that carries through the rest of my day.

In order to make this work in your own life, Dr. Newport says you need to understand the act of focusing. He compares it to doing a pull-up (which is where you hang from a bar and pull your body weight up so your chin clears the bar)—both are easy to understand but very hard to do without training. The way you would train your body to be strong enough to pull itself up to a bar is the same way you would train your mind to be able to focus without distraction—practise, practise, practise, and then practise some more.

Dr. Newport suggests that you do 10 focus sessions for a particular length of time (say, 10 to 20 minutes) before you add another 10 minutes to the clock. That's how slow it is to increase the ability to focus, which is why, no matter how committed you are to smashing that first 4% hour, without preparation and, yes, training, it will be tough for you to maintain your focus.

Ideally, after you rise and shine, you will get that full 60 minutes to be "head down" on something that is meaningful and exciting for you. However, this is likely unrealistic, particularly in the beginning. I'm a seasoned 4% fix pro, and I still struggle some mornings to keep myself focused and on task.

Research on corporate work environments also shows that most of us can focus for only *minutes* at a time before we break away to do something else, and that it can take us three times as long to get back to the task at hand. So, armed with this knowledge and awareness—but also acknowledging that I don't have a Ph.D. and my sample size is N=1—here's some non-scientific advice for how I've personally made it work: *one tiny chunk of time at a time.*

PART FOUR: ENJOY YOUR TIME (THE POINT OF IT ALL)

*Our goals can only be reached through a vehicle of a plan,
in which we must fervently believe, and upon which we must
vigorously act. There is no other route to success.*
—Pablo Picasso

DARE TO BE IDLE

Life can only take place in the present moment.
—BUDDHA

There is nothing quite like a global pandemic to force you to slow down. When COVID-19 hit the world, spreading across countries with breathtaking speed, it seemed we went from normal life to isolation lockdown in a matter of days. As happened for millions of others, many of my daily, predictable rituals disappeared. Even though, as a work-from-home writer, I spend much of my day on my own, I could always escape to the library or a coffee shop if I needed a change in work scenery. Suddenly, my normally quiet house (my office) was full of other humans, who like me were struggling to find a rhythm in this new normal.

Our 12-year-old wasn't in school, and we were expected to do some homeschooling—a disaster for all involved, if I'm being completely honest. My husband, whose physiotherapy clinics closed to help stop the spread of the virus, suddenly found himself with vast amounts of unplanned and stressful time on his hands.

For many others—front-line workers, grocery store attendants, government officials—this period was the opposite of slamming a foot on the brake. Their work expanded to frightening levels. But for the rest of us? There was time to just *do nothing*. Which was a mindf*ck for those of us used to squeezing our days bone-dry. Sure, you could still fill your days if you wanted or needed to. Along with detailed grocery item cleaning rituals and homemade mask sewing, people started online workshops, art modules, cooking tutorials, reading clubs, and live-streamed exercise classes. A host of people in my social streams binge-watched Netflix shows they hadn't had time for, or read classics that had been sitting on their bookshelves for years.

But even within these varying degrees of "pandemic productivity" there were going to be pockets of time that simply couldn't be filled. Periods where you were forced to be idle because the pantry was pristine, all your socks had found their matches, and you were caught up on Netflix. For some, like me, this state of idleness is the most uncomfortable of all. I am not great at existing in the present moment. I remain a work in progress with my attempts at mindfulness and meditation. The reason I *want* to become a crackerjack meditator, despite quieting my mind being Mensa-level tough, is that as a journalist who reads a lot of magazine and newspaper articles, I am well aware of the benefits of mindfulness. "The present is a present" and "Be where your feet are" are lovely, enviable concepts that sound straightforward but in reality are not.

Over the past few years, the world has offered plenty of newfangled ways to streamline and declutter our lives. From KonMari to *hygge* (pronounced "hoo-ga," and Danish for "cozy"), we have been promised simplicity, joy, and clarity. Yet we are also required to *do more* in order to reap those benefits. I can only speak for myself, but the weekend I spent rolling socks, thanking my clothes, and trying to fit IKEA baskets Jenga-style into my drawers was neither joyful nor simple. I kept thinking, *Why am I doing this again?* as I tried to remember the precise KonMari order I needed to follow to trim my closets.

Perhaps instead I should have spent that weekend slacking off—which, according to a 2014 paper ("Doing Nothing and Nothing to Do: The Hidden Value of Empty Time and Boredom," by psychoanalyst Manfred Kets de Vries) may be "the best thing we can do for our mental health." Kets de Vries says that during periods of inactivity (slacking off counts), the right hemisphere of our brain, which is the workhorse for meditation, daydreaming, creative endeavours, and imagination, has the opportunity to express itself. While we're busy doing all the things, our left hemisphere is especially occupied with managing logic, analytical thought, reasoning, and language, and so it calls on the right hemisphere to lighten the load. When we are idle, or bored, the left hemisphere is less needed and the right hemisphere seizes its chance to shine.

Have you ever had a brilliant idea or solved what felt like an unsolvable problem in the shower, or just before falling asleep, or maybe when you're sitting alone in nature? The quietness and stillness of your mind during these types of activities allows for thought processes that couldn't get through the noise before.

Our brains never really shut down. Even when we're practising meditation and mindfulness, and even when we're sleeping. They remain in action, every hour of every day. This brings me to the lifestyle concept of *niksen*, a gift from the Dutch, which means "to do nothing." If mindfulness is about being present, then *niksen* is about simply being. When you "*niks*," you are letting your mind wander. It looks like sitting on the couch staring into space, or maybe you're on the couch but doing a low-focus task such as knitting, or walking through the woods. There is no purpose to *niksen* aside from putting in idle time.

A 2013 *Frontiers in Psychology* study on the pros and cons of mind-wandering found that when we *niks*, it helps us harness inspiration and clarity about actions we need to take to meet our future goals. *So doing nothing is the key to doing something.* Imagine that.

If sitting on the couch and staring into space feels like too much of nothing—and the exuberantly productive sorts reading this are sure to feel that way—there are ways to benefit from this act of being without having to go full tilt. Find a quiet spot and write in a gratitude journal. Go for a walk along a river or on a beach. Throw a bath bomb into a hot bath, dim the lights, and enjoy the float.

But before you do something, first learn to do nothing.

THE PROBLEM WITH PASSION

Spread joy. Chase your wildest dreams.
—PATCH ADAMS

To say Karl Meltzer likes to run would be a massive understatement. At 52 years old, "Speedgoat" Meltzer's running bio is pretty extraordinary. Thinking about it makes me feel lazy and makes my knees hurt. As of 2019, Meltzer had won thirty-eight 100-mile runs, making him the winningest 100-mile runner on earth. The Appalachian Trail (a.k.a. the A.T.), a 2,200-mile footpath trail that ranges from Maine to Georgia, takes the average backpacker five to seven months to complete—and it should be noted that only 20% of hikers who start the trail actually finish it. In 2016 Meltzer ran the entirety of the A.T., finishing in 45 days, 22 hours, and 38 minutes—a record-breaking time that makes him the fastest ever to complete it. Clearly long-distance running doesn't faze him, as he's also won 52 ultramarathons (which is basically any distance over the standard 26.2-mile marathon, and can be as long as 1,000 miles). If you wanted to see passion play out in real time, this is it: Karl Meltzer embodies the very definition of passion, which according to Merriam-Webster is "devotion to some activity, object or concept."

In cases like Karl Meltzer's, passion is obvious. Similarly minded is Danielle Steel, the novelist who has written nearly 200 books. Steel works 20 to 22 hours a day (she sleeps about 4 hours per night, she says), and basically spends more time writing than on anything else in her life, even though she has *nine* children. Danielle Steel has a lucrative career, enough books to fill a small-town library on her own, and clearly loves writing. She has dedicated her entire life to her craft—she takes a single one-week vacation per year— and the results of her passion and drive are evidenced in her *New York Times* bestseller records and the sheer volume of work she's produced. As with Meltzer, this is passion in action. And while it's impressive and perhaps even enviable (Steel releases seven novels or so a year and is at work on multiple projects at a time), it's also the result of an extraordinary commitment and enormous sacrifices, and is nearly impossible to replicate. Some of us have that insane level of drive; most of us do not.

For that "most" of us, passion is simply too big an idea, not dissimilar to the notion of a BHAG. It's a sweeping concept that (as we've seen with the earlier examples) demands a significant commitment—on multiple fronts—for the rewards it provides. But it should be noted that you can be passionate about something without it having to be a "big P Passion," or even a career, for that matter. Case in point: my husband is passionate about skiing. He has been doing it since he could walk and would probably ski every day of the year if he could. It brings him joy in a way that isn't easy to find elsewhere. Similarly, I'm passionate about books and reading. There are many things I would give up before I gave up books. I have spent *years* of my life reading, if I were to add up all the hours, and as my husband does when skiing down a mountain, I feel a simple but resounding joy when I have a great book in hand and an empty afternoon in which to read it . . . *Bliss.*

But unlike Karl Meltzer or Danielle Steel or any other person who has committed their life to focusing on one specific thing, I juggle a lot more than reading—even though being a professional reader, if that were a thing, sounds like a pretty great way to spend one's life. Being *passionate* and being *dedicated to a passion* are not the same thing, which is a critical difference to keep in mind when brainstorming how to spend that first 4% of your day . . . especially if you factor in a 5 a.m. (or so) alarm. Getting up super early, only to be unclear about the reason *why*, is a recipe for a less-than-happy start to your day.

Despite the clear differences between passion as an emotion versus passion as a calling, there is plenty of well-meaning advice to be found on the issue. This advice often touts uncovering your passion as the gateway to success and happiness. There are many related memes to iron onto T-shirts (or print on a coffee mug if, like me, that's more your jam), things like "Follow Your Bliss" or "Soar with

Your Joy" or "Practice Your Passion." All of these mantras sound inspiring and wonderful. Who doesn't want to soar with their joy? A host of things make me blissful, including chocolate-covered jujubes and hunting for beach shells and walking along a snow-covered forest trail. Yet, from a practical standpoint, what exactly does it look like to "follow your bliss?"

Is this "find your passion" advice helping anyone?

If you haven't watched the famous commencement speech Steve Jobs gave at Stanford University in 2015, in which he addresses the concept of passion, it can be summed up by his statement that "You've got to find what you love . . . if you haven't found it yet, don't settle." That speech has been viewed 34 million times on YouTube, which means a lot of people have heard—and likely taken to heart—Jobs's advice on finding your passion. In response, our friend Dr. Newport addressed Jobs's comments, and said that, from his viewpoint, this is common but also "astonishingly bad" advice. He follows this up with Newport's Law (making a quip in his presentation that the only reason to go into science is to name laws after yourself), which states, "Telling a young person to follow their passion reduces the probability they will end up passionate." I would argue this could be true for all people, not just the young ones.

About a decade ago, I discovered that I loved writing fiction. Could we call my writing a "passion"? Probably— though maybe the "small *p*" variety, because I certainly appreciate vacations and can't imagine publishing more than a book a year. But I didn't uncover this passion until my mid-30s, and only after considering and testing out other enterprises first. Dr. Newport suggests that while you *should* be passionate about what you do, "clearly identified, pre-existing passions are rare." More often than not, our passions evolve more slowly over time.

"Follow your passion" also presupposes you have a passion you *can* follow, and you might not be there yet. If I think about the people in my life—both those I know well and others I've merely crossed paths with, particularly in my industry—I can come up with only a handful who have a blatant passion that lives at the centre of everything they do, driving their behaviours, decisions, and goals.

But back to Steve Jobs for a moment. It's easy to see he was passionate about technology entrepreneurship; his enormous success and singular focus prove that. But he actually stumbled into Apple, and it was then that his enthusiasm for it grew. So really, what's important is probably not how you get started—or if you're able to label a passion right out of the gate—but what you do once you get going. Even those who have an obvious skill for something, like Danielle Steel and Karl Meltzer, must also have a great love for the thing they've chosen to do; otherwise it settles into a hobby rather than a "calling."

Think about what tickles your curiosity, what piques your interest, without requiring you to ditch everything else in your life to spend most of your days becoming a master at it. Curiosity is less robust than passion—it is shorter-term (though it could always lead to passion eventually) and most definitely worth exploring. Give that thing you're curious about a try, because even if you decide it's not the right thing for you in the end, the investment of time, energy, and effort will have been minimal in the grand scheme. This is a perfect example of "What do I have to lose?"

KNOW THYSELF

Nothing in the universe ever grew from the outside in.
—Richard Wagamese

When I was 17 years old, I attended a program with Outward Bound that was described as an "outdoor education" but from my experience felt more like traipsing through the *Hunger Games* landscape. It was no joke—I spent a month in the woods, basically becoming more feral every day. We had to shake out our sleeping bags each night to be sure no snakes had snuggled in. We once canoed for about 15 hours (we were lost, in a vast series of lakes), stopping only to carry heavy packs and equipment across bogs and up rugged trails long overgrown. I wore the same pair of shorts and two T-shirts for a month, and went weeks without washing my hair or seeing indoor plumbing. I also, for the first and last time of my life, ate canned sardines and so many peanuts (via GORP, good old raisins and peanuts trail mix) that I ended up developing a peanut allergy by the end of it.

It was also *so much fun*, and one of the best experiences of my life.

There were a lot of firsts for me during that month, including watching a bull moose walk straight through our camp, kayaking rapids, building latrines, and running with sled dogs. It was also when I was introduced to the idea of a bucket list. After I got home, I started a list of all the things I wanted to accomplish or experience. At last check, 30 years later, the list now has 87 items on it. A whole bunch have been checked off and plenty more added, and I have been working and thinking about that list for decades.

One of the first things I wrote down was to go skydiving. A couple of things to know about me: I don't love airplanes and I really like being alive. So you might wonder why I put skydiving on the list, and all I can say is, back then I was young enough to believe I was invincible. I figured I would simply do it *later*—like, maybe on a significant birthday, like my 90th, when I felt I had lived a most excellent life and so, if my parachute didn't open, well, fine then.

As I was approaching my 40th birthday, I took a good look at the list, wondering what I might be able to check off as a birthday gift to myself. And near the top I saw *Skydiving*. Now, generally if I say I'm going to do something, there's about a 98% chance I will. But as I considered that list and imagined jumping out of a plane . . . *nope*. Instead, I went indoor skydiving with my family, which, while still thrilling and exciting, also ensured the whole "I like being alive" thing. It only requires the courage to get suited up and step into the air chamber, "flying" at most 10 feet above the ground. After my birthday I checked that one right off my bucket list, not even bothering to add *Indoor* in front of *Skydiving*.

When you're thinking about waking early for that 4% fix, and about what excites you enough that it will be possible to do so without anger, resentment, weeping, or fear of death, I offer this advice: *Know thyself.*

It may seem obvious that self-awareness—a consciousness of one's own personality and individuality and feelings—is critical here. After all, choosing to get up early for something that doesn't resonate with your inner self means it's unlikely you're ever going to put in the time needed to see it through. Yet we are so busy-minded these days, it can feel like our ability to be self-aware has gone soft—do we even know what we *really* want anymore? Not only are many of us dealing with jam-packed schedules and a heck of a lot of adulting, we also have, literally at our fingertips, 24-7, the ability to disengage with our inner selves. Our smartphones and other devices are a constant source of feedback, telling us with beeps and whistles and vibrations what and whom we should pay attention to. But while they keep us informed and on track, they also confuse the hell out of our self-awareness.

For example, I know with 100% certainty I do not like smoothie bowls. No, thank you—I stand by my belief that smoothies are for drinking, not eating with a spoon, and certainly should not be cluttered with chunks of fruit and granola and coconut chips and, good grief, the super-trendy (but what are they, *really?*) hemp hearts and chia seeds. However, Instagram makes smoothie bowls look not only delicious but necessary. As a result, I question my hatred of smoothie bowls on a near daily basis.

How connected are you feeling right now to your inner self? Is your smartphone messing not only with your self-awareness, but also with your time? For a device that should make our lives easier and more efficient, the smart-phone has turned out to be one of the greatest time sucks of, well, all time. Nothing has been more enlightening for me than the social media check screen, which keeps a running tally of the number of hours you've spent that day on your social apps, etc. (and if you dig deeper, how many times you pick up your phone every hour). It has been sobering some days, but I resist the urge to turn it off because, while it typ-ically makes me feel defensive, the reality is that much of the time I spend scrolling through and popping into social feeds has no value whatsoever.

A Pew Research Center survey from January 2018 found about a quarter (26%) of adults in the United States are online "almost constantly" and 77% are online at least daily. Ever feel your cellphone buzz, or hear the sound of its vibration, only to pull it out and realize there was no notification? No text, no email, nothing from your social media platforms? Remember phantom vibration syndrome? It's a real thing and apparently affects enough of us that studies are now being dedicated to the phenomenon. While it might seem like no big deal, that constant connection to our phones— and this sense that they need to be within arm's length—it certainly messes with our focus and with what some refer to as "mindfulness": that ability to shut everything else off and check in with the *present* moment (and not the present moment on Twitter).

Committing to a 4% fix is partly about forcing that break. Your device may be a critical element of how you choose to spend your hour (say, watching online videos to learn to play the guitar), but its use should be focused and controlled, so your precious time doesn't get eaten up.

While it might feel counterproductive, I believe an important part of the "know thyself" strategy is to also be clear about what you *don't* want to do with any hidden time you can uncover (like jump out of an airplane). Here's my short list of things I never want to tackle, no matter how much time I have:

1. Becoming stock market savvy.

2. Learning to play an instrument.

3. DIY-ing in any way—this includes crafting and making my own sourdough starter.

4. Writing poetry.

5. Barefoot waterskiing (because . . . why?).

What's on your list of "no, thanks, I'm good" activities or experiences? It's okay to admit that not everything is your cup of tea. Your path to the things you're excited about doing is much better landscaped once you cut back on the stuff you don't want to do.

STOP MAKING EXCUSES

The walls of your comfort zone are lovingly decorated
with your lifelong collection of favorite excuses.
—JEN SINCERO

'd like to tell you about two women I knew who each had a book in them they one day hoped to publish. The first was a whip-smart and talented editor friend named Tracy, who had worked at *Today's Parent*—a Toronto-based national parenting magazine—for 14 years, and who I was lucky enough to collaborate with on a few articles. Tracy was a mom, wife, editor, educator, writer, and all-around excellent person—who was also incredibly busy with the things most adults must do on a daily basis.

I first met Tracy at a conference focused on blogging, back when "mommy bloggers" were everywhere (I was one of them), and she was running a panel on pitching and writing for magazines. She was nervous, I could tell, mostly because she was the sort of person who wanted to be helpful. Tracy had worked hard on her presentation and was genuinely hopeful it would lead the keen writers in the room to come up with successful pitching strategies. We chatted after the panel, about writing, about magazine work (I gave her a soft pitch for an article I would later write for *Today's Parent*), and about fiction, which was something I was working on in the early hours of the morning but hadn't yet found an agent or publisher for. Tracy also had the beginnings of a novel—romance, with a still fairly loose plot—and we excitedly discussed the challenges of writing fiction, especially when life was *so very busy*. I told her about my 5 a.m. writing habit and, like many others, she was equal parts impressed and certain she could never wake up early to write. "Fair enough," I said. "It's not for everyone."

A couple of years and a handful of articles later, Tracy and I exchanged our last emails on April 23, 2015. I had pitched a blog idea, and she wanted to update me that it was a go but had been passed to a different editor. I asked about her fiction writing. She wrote back: *There is no progress with the fiction! Though I do have a character that I develop while sitting in meetings . . .* Tracy went on to say her plan had been to dive into the book after finishing up teaching in March (she thought she'd have all this extra time, as we do when we imagine a project ending . . . forgetting that another one usually takes its place if we don't hold that slot), but there was a "side project" that was massive and time-consuming and had an end-of-April deadline. She congratulated me on my first book, which would be published four months later, and I said I hoped she'd be able to come to the launch party.

Sometime during the evening of May 18, 2015, Tracy died in bed—suddenly and unexpectedly. She was 41 and had suffered a brain aneurysm, leaving behind her husband and two young daughters, a legacy of stories through the pages of *Today's Parent*, family and friends who would miss her desperately, and an unfinished novel.

I've often thought about Tracy in the years since. Of that novel she desperately wanted to finish but could never find the time for. I wish she had been able to—I wish I had read it, even unfinished, so I could have congratulated her on getting as far as she had. It's no small thing to write a book, even if you're only partway done.

Michele Bosc helped run Château des Charmes winery with her husband and his family in the Niagara-on-the-Lake region. She was as passionate about wine as she was about hard rock music and driving her sports car fast and being a mother and supporting women to succeed. I met Michele via Twitter, and she asked me if I'd have lunch with her so she could "pick my brain" about publishing. We had a lovely lunch—she was a firecracker of a person with a huge laugh and an abundance of energy—and I learned she was writing an erotic romance set in the wine region of Niagara. It sounded fun and salacious, and I told her I looked forward to reading it one day.

We stayed in touch, and the last time I saw her, at a book event for my latest novel at her winery, she told me she had recently finished part two of what had turned into an erotic romance series. This was impressive because, along with everything else, she was in the midst of cancer treatment (for the third time). A two-time cancer survivor with a deep respect for the "life is short" mantra, Michele was not one to procrastinate on her goals—something else we had in common. In between her day job and parenting her son and all the other commitments she had, she wrote those erotic romances. She asked for feedback and took it to heart, never being precious about her writing. She hired a professional editor once she had taken the book as far as she could on her own.

After four years and many rewrites to turn her original idea into an actual book, Michele self-published her debut novel—the first in the series—one month before she died, at only 52, from complications from her cancer.

It's easy to make excuses. To put things off for another day. There is a good chance for most of us that we are going to get that other day. So we have the luxury of procrastination, of pushing goals and "one day I hope to . . ." wishes to a later, ideally less busy date in the calendar. But here's the thing: if you have something you want to do, go figure out how to do it. With urgency and purpose.

I can't tell you the number of times someone has said to me, "Oh, I would love to write a book. But I don't have the time!" When they ask how I find the time to write, I tell them it's often at 5 a.m., and they narrow their eyes and shake their heads. "I could never do that." *Yeah, you could.*

There will always be a reason why you can't find the time. Kids. Jobs. Family. The house. Sleep. Lack of inspiration. Lack of skill. Fear of failure. Fear of success. The list is endless, and the reality is that most of us excel at coming up with reasons why things remain out of reach.

So maybe it's time to flip that around. Find reasons *to do* that thing you've always wanted to and have been putting off (perhaps without realizing it). And while an illness, loss, or scare of some sort *can* be an effective kick in the pants, the idea of being proactive versus reactive is much more appealing. As Edward R. Murrow, a broadcast journalist during World War II, said, "Difficulty is the excuse history never accepts."

A WORD ON CREATIVITY

*Creativity itself doesn't care at all about results—
the only thing it craves is the process. Learn to love
the process and let whatever happens next happen,
without fussing too much about it.*
—Elizabeth Gilbert

This is the story about how a painting titled *Pepper-corn Butt* saved my creativity on a day when I really needed it. There's a Chicago-area artist and art teacher, Amanda Evanston Freund, whom I discovered on Instagram through a friend, and who creates gorgeous, dynamic paintings I wish could adorn every room in my home. Recently she posted a photo of one of her pieces, along with the story behind it. The artwork—a stunning 11-by-14 acrylic and NuPastel done on paper—had a title that caught my attention. *Peppercorn Butt*. At first glance, its title, in my mind, didn't exactly fit. The painting was abstractly floral, with

215

a kaleidoscope of pinks, oranges, and reds, and with some black ink-blot-style paint marks speckled throughout. As I zoomed in, taking a closer look at it, I decided those black ink blots were the peppercorns, and I found a somewhat frowny face (abstract; again, possibly just my brain seeing something that wasn't really there) buried in one of the petals. Then, curiosity piqued, I read the story Amanda had written about how the piece came to fruition, which went as follows:

> The other day I was at the grocery store and dropped a spice jar on the ground. It shattered so hard that the lady 15' down the aisle *screamed* because she felt a peppercorn hit her in the butt like a bullet. She was very kind about it, though. Even got down and helped me pick up some remnants. As I was on my hands and knees with her trying to pick up the broken glass pieces and spice bits, it occurred to me that if I was shot in the butt with a peppercorn, I likely would not be half so nice about it. I probably would have been peeved and stormed off. I would have blamed her for my pain and pointed a finger, at least in my head. It was humbling to think she would show me grace that I might not have allowed her. I don't know what I'm saying here, but moments like this matter. They really do.

When I came across Amanda's artwork I was actively procrastinating. My attention was supposed to be focused on writing a chapter on creativity—*this* chapter, in fact—which should have been a snap to write (I deal in creativity all day long) but was proving to be anything but. So I was aimlessly scrolling Instagram, as one does, past the smoothie bowls when *Peppercorn Butt* caught my eye. I reached out to Amanda to ask about the painting (it was already sold) and learned that her painting titles all come from an anecdote she's heard or experienced. Something that inspires the art as she makes it. She explained that she names each piece on the back, before she lays any paint on the canvas, adding, "Trying to relay abstract or complicated feelings into 2D paint is what makes it art."

If you scroll through Amanda's Instagram feed, you'll see *Peppercorn Butt* isn't a one-off: each of her paintings comes with a unique, at times laugh-inducing or heart-tugging name and a story to go with it. Like her series called The Friend, which includes *The Friend Who Likes John Stamos a Little Too Much* and *The Friend Who Thinks Your Weird Hammer Toe Is Cute* and *The Friend Who Took Your Mom to Chemo When You Had to Work.* There are also pieces called *Splendour in the Shoe Section, Jam Jar Party on the Lawn,* and my personal favourite, *A Happy Birthday for Walter the Omelet Loving Basset Hound.*

Amanda is one of those people we might label a (capital *C*) Creative. I mean, who can take a story about a smashed glass peppercorn jar in the grocery store and turn it into a beautiful piece of showcase art that somehow *also* manages to capture an experience? Someone damn creative, that's who. As an author, I am often asked about creativity—or more specifically, how do I take a two-line premise and turn it into an 85,000-word novel in which the character, world, and details feel so real? Creativity and imagination, that's how!

But creativity isn't something you have or don't have. In many ways, it's actually an acquired skill, developed with practice and a willingness to fail spectacularly, to take a leap and do something when you aren't yet sure what the outcome might be. If you have any sort of imagination (spoiler alert: we *all* do) you have the capacity for creativity.

Furthermore, creativity is not as magical as it may seem. Sure, science highlights a few notable differences between a "creative" person and a more analytical one. The brains of creatives tend to be smaller, actually, but they have more networks stretching between the left and right hemispheres. And those networks, those pathways, are what allow us to tap into greater creativity—to imagine the world differently from the way we currently see or experience it.

Human beings are the only species capable of being creative in this way. If you've ever seen a delicate and intricate paper wasp nest, or a spiderweb that has captured the early-morning dew, you feel you've witnessed something artistic and creative. But the ability to transform the current world with our minds, often for the sheer enjoyment of it rather than for any practical reason, is what sets us apart from the rest of the animal kingdom.

If the project you want to tackle trends more traditionally creative—say, writing a book or learning to paint or making some other type of art or playing an instrument— and you feel you don't have a creative bone in your body, do not despair. You just have to poke at your creativity a little, to wake it up and tell it, "Time to show up!" Easier said than done, but it *can* be done.

One of the best ways to call upon your creativity is to ignore the voice in your head that tells you this is not a skill that's available to you. As well, try not to apply too much force—your creativity knows when it's being manhandled, and it doesn't care for that. So rather than going into a project with anxiety about the finished product, or about whether you can be creative enough to accomplish it, or perhaps comparing yourself to someone who you believe is über-creative in doing the very thing you're attempting, you need to relax and go with the flow. This might mean journaling an idea you've always had for a novel, writing down snippets of the story that have come to you and then expanding on them in a free-form style of writing that doesn't box in your imagination (like being bound by consecutive chapters, for example). Maybe it's pulling out some paints and a watercolour pad and experimenting with how the colours fit together, without a plan for what it "needs" to look like when you're done. Kids are the best at this, so if you have one in your life, take a cue from them: they typically don't care much about the end result and are there for the fun of the experience. My daughter has a ukulele, and before she started to learn proper notes and songs through school, she would strum the strings and make up a song as she went, with no concern for how it sounded or if the song made sense (it didn't, usually, but she didn't care).

In the well-known book *The Artist's Way*—on the bookshelf of nearly every creative I know—author Julia Cameron offers strategies and exercises to "awaken" the creativity inside you. For those who are feeling stuck, she provides exercises to help you recover your creativity when it feels as though it has gone into hibernation. Interestingly, Cameron originally self-published *The Artist's Way* (she typed out and Xeroxed the copies of the book herself, in the early 1990s) before it was picked up by a publisher and went on to sell millions of copies.

In her book, Cameron suggests using what she calls "morning pages," which essentially means stream-of-consciousness journaling, ideally done first thing in the morning. It can be about any topic you want to write about or work through—the idea being, it helps push you past the fear and lockdown of feeling non-creative (you're creating with every paragraph you write, because you're literally bringing words to the page that weren't there before) and gets you into the habit of letting your creative juices flow.

Now, journaling is not for everyone. I will admit I've tried the morning pages approach, and the stream-of-consciousness journaling frustrates me. So instead, I write about something specific, like a character dilemma or a setting description or something that feels like it has forward momentum for the particular story I'm working on. But the *habit* of it is the key, as is the release from fear. That is more powerful than anything—if you're afraid to see what you might be able to create, you are limiting yourself unnecessarily.

GROUNDHOG DAY

It is never too late to be what you might have been.
—GEORGE ELIOT

When I first saw the 1993 movie *Groundhog Day*, starring Bill Murray and Andie MacDowell, I was around 21 years old. I was a decade away from being married and 14 years away from having a kid, and I thought the movie was hilarious and fun, and it became one of those films I watched every time it showed up on television. If you're much younger than I am and haven't seen it, here's the basic premise: weatherman Phil Connors (Murray) is sent to cover the annual Groundhog Day celebration in Punxsutawney, Pennsylvania, and inexplicably ends up in a bizarre time loop, reliving the same day over and over again. The movie led to the phrase "It feels like Groundhog Day every day," a sentiment I didn't fully appreciate until I became a mother. Because when you're knee-deep in parenting, you can begin to feel like Bill Murray in *Groundhog Day*.

When it's hard to imagine your days as anything other than a continuous, repetitive loop—and, of course, you might feel this way for a hundred different reasons—it's also hard to see what's possible in terms of starting something new. How can you take on anything else when your day is chockablock as it is? I started writing in earnest in my late 30s and got my agent just before I turned 40. That placed me firmly in the "middle-aged" category, and I often questioned the sanity of uprooting my own personal Groundhog Day (while frustrating, it was also predictable) for something unknown. But I wanted to be published, and the only way to do that was to write a book. And the only way to write a book, given the other stuff I had to do each and every day, was to get up at 5 a.m.

For anyone in the "I'm too old to start something new" camp, here are a few famous examples proving how untrue that really is. Case one: Colonel Sanders, who started the "finger lickin' good" Kentucky Fried Chicken (KFC) in the 1930s. As the story goes, Sanders had been fired from a series of jobs. At the age of 40, he bought a Shell service station and then started cooking chicken out of it—during the Great Depression, no less. He spent 10 years perfecting KFC's "secret recipe," which was even praised by food critic Duncan Hines (yes, that Duncan Hines, of boxed cake fame), yet despite his entrepreneurial drive and the glowing praise for his now renowned chicken recipe, he went broke and was forced to close his business and retire in the 1950s. However, undeterred, Sanders set out to find restaurants that would franchise his chicken, asking for a nickel for each piece of chicken sold. It's said he slept in his car and was rejected more than 1,000 times before finding his first partner. KFC is now the second-largest fast-food chain (after McDonald's), and its brand is worth $8.5 billion. Not bad for a guy who decided to forge a new path in "middle-age."

Case two: Julia "Hurricane" Hawkins, who took up running—literally became a first-time runner—at the age of 100. The former schoolteacher started running because she could no longer bike, and then decided it would be "neat to run at 100 and do the 100-yard dash." I mean, why the hell not, right? Whoever let a century-old body stop them from doing anything? In 2019, at the spritely age of 103, Hawkins continued her training by gardening on her acre of land. It seemed to work, as she subsequently won gold at the 2019 National Senior Games for running the 100-metre dash in an impressive 46.07 seconds. For some perspective, the average adult female can run 100 metres in 34 seconds (the average man, 27 seconds), and Olympian Usain Bolt holds the world record for the fastest 100-metre dash, at 9.58 seconds (a cheetah can do it in 5.95 seconds, and a racehorse in 5.1 seconds).

Finally, case three: Carl Allamby, a 47-year-old Cleveland man who recently started his residency after having enrolled in medical school at the age of 40. What makes Allamby's story particularly compelling is that he only had a 2.0 GPA in high school but went on to start a body shop business (he ended up owning a couple of garages) and became a successful entrepreneur—all before doing a career switcheroo in his forties. As a child he had wanted to be a doctor, so he ultimately decided he wanted to try medicine. He found a mentor and then applied and got in to medical school, even as he cared for his young family. Allamby now works at the Cleveland Clinic Akron General Hospital in emergency medicine. Some might say age 40 is too late to start something so significant—the sheer number of years one has to be in school to become a physician can be overwhelming at any age, especially when juggling a family. Of course, if you constantly tell yourself it's too late, well, chances are you're going to end up believing it and changing nothing until it is indeed too late.

While these are more extreme examples of late-in-the-day change-ups, you do not need to completely uproot your life to reap the benefits of breaking out of Groundhog Day. Say you've always dreamed of learning to speak Italian (preferably while also scootering through the Tuscan countryside, of course); while it might be ideal to move to Florence and immerse yourself in the culture and country, that may not be practical, or possible, during this stage of life. But you could absolutely set an alarm for 5 a.m. a couple of days a week (or every morning, if you can swing it), put those earbuds in and listen to a Rosetta Stone program.

Remember what Daniel H. Pink identified about our brains and the clock: our brains are best suited to focused work in the morning. As further ammunition for a 4% fix alarm, Pink also found that afternoons are pretty much the worst time to do anything important—anesthesia errors, for example, are four times more likely at 3 p.m. than at 9 a.m., and a study done on students in Denmark found that those who took standardized tests in the morning did significantly better than those who took them in the afternoon.

If the morning is the bee's-knees time for learning something new—which inevitably requires more focus, as you don't have experience or history to guide you—then setting that early alarm is the first step in breaking out of your rut and saying goodbye to Groundhog Day.

PUT IT INTO PRACTICE

Talent is a pursued interest. Anything that you're
willing to practice, you can do.
—BOB ROSS

E very spring in New York City, a competition takes place that would blow most of our minds. It's the USA Memory Championship, where competitors (called memory athletes) from around the world congregate to perform such feats as memorizing 117 names and faces, or a list of 200 words, in only 15 minutes, or as many digits as possible in a mere 5 minutes. The 2019 winner was Lance Tschirhart, who holds the U.S. record for memorizing an unbelievable 360 digits in 5 minutes. That's like memorizing 51 phone numbers in about the time it takes to unload the dishwasher.

Now, some might think these memory athletes have bigger brains, are smarter, and have memory capabilities that border on superpowers, but science has proven that's simply not true. When memory athletes were tested against other test subjects in functional MRI machines, researchers found two interesting things: one, the memory athletes and test subjects were similar in terms of brain size and other measures of intelligence; and two, certain areas of the memory athletes' brains (but not the other test subjects'), notably the areas related to navigation and spatial awareness, lit up while they were performing the tasks. The memory athletes were different, but it turns out it wasn't about intelligence or some sort of freak-of-nature memory skills; it was about process and practice.

As someone who feels she has a mediocre memory, I was astounded by what these folks could do. But memory masters all say they are not special—they simply use ancient memory techniques and a whole lot of practice, incorporating things like meditation, which has been shown to help the brain focus.

Among these techniques to improve memory and retain an impressive number of details quickly exists one of the most discussed and revered: the concept of a memory palace. A memory palace is an imaginary location in your mind (like your own house or neighbourhood) where you can store mental images to remember facts, numbers, and other details. So, for example, if I wanted to remember my husband's new cellphone number, I might close my eyes and imagine our house, then more specifically his white car parked in our garage, and with my mind draw the numbers on the car's hood in thick black paint.

The idea is to create a visual representation of what you're trying to remember—and experts say the more absurd or emotionally relevant it is the better—so when you go to retrieve it, you'll reimagine the mental picture and the data will be easier to recall. My husband adores his car, and putting black paint on its white hood would obviously generate a lively discussion, so the visual (and therefore, the phone number) definitely sticks with me.

If you still don't believe anyone could learn to do this, let me tell you about science journalist Joshua Foer. A decade or so ago Foer ended up at the USA Memory Championship and learned firsthand how these memory athletes trained. He was intrigued. Could *he* train his memory the way these athletes did? In the true spirit of participatory journalism, he started applying the techniques, like creating a memory palace, to his own memory. A year later he decided to compete (for fun, he said) in the USA Memory Championship, and he won—proving that with the right amount of determination and dedication (daily practice was involved), any one of us can become a memory master. Furthermore, Foer's story shows that if you decide you want something, and figure out how to fit it into your day-to-day life, you can go from "I wonder if I could . . ." to "I smashed that!"

What does becoming a memory master have to do with getting up at 5 a.m.? I talk to a lot of people who are intrigued by my morning lark writing habit but don't think they have the capability to do it themselves. As if, somehow, I am uniquely skilled at waking up early and setting my fingers atop my laptop keys to generate prose. I assure you I am not. Like the memory masters, it's something I am committed to and practise almost every day. Which means it looks effortless, even though that's not at all the case.

I'm here to tell you I whined a lot in the early days of my 5 a.m. writer's club journey. I felt tired, and frustrated, and often wished I could just go back to bed. I'm sure Joshua Foer also felt frustrated, and tired, and often wished he didn't have to wear—for hours—the special DIY goggles (which are blacked out except for a pinpoint for each eye) and earmuffs to practise memorization while blocking out distractions.

I've said it before, and I'll say it again: getting up earlier than you currently do is simple, though not easy. Which is why, no matter what you decide to get out of bed for, you'll want to be sure it's something that (a) you are excited about; (b) won't overextend your abilities or resources; and (c) brings you "job well done" satisfaction once you master it.

THIS IS AN EXPERIMENT

Remember that sometimes not getting what you want is a wonderful stroke of luck.
—DALAI LAMA

In 1905 in San Francisco, an 11-year-old kid named Frank Epperson was attempting to make his own soft drink. He mixed soda water powder with water (a common beverage back then) and left it on the back porch overnight. It was a surprisingly cold night, and when Frank woke up in the morning, he found the mixture had frozen overnight— with the stir stick still in it. It would be another 15 years before he decided to patent his creation, but that frozen cup of soda water powder ended up being the birth of what we now know as the Popsicle.

This is only one example of an experiment that led to a happy accident and resulted in an invention we can't imagine living without. Like **microwave ovens** (while working with microwaves, the inventor of the microwave oven discovered that a chocolate bar melted in his pocket and decided to see what else those rays could heat up); **Play-Doh** (it was originally created to clean coal soot off wallpaper); **Velcro** (the inventor noticed burrs on his dog's fur after a hike and started experimenting with hook-and-loop combinations); **Coca-Cola** (it was first concocted as a headache remedy); and the antibiotic **penicillin**. The common thread among all of these inventions is not how life-altering they have been (even though that is a fact), but how low-risk each of them was. There was no BHAG to ratchet up the tension, and each discovery was merely a by-product of another experiment—hence, zero disappointment or sense of failure.

However, we all know there are plenty of things that can derail even BHAG-free projects or experiments. One such derailment may come in the form of the voice in your head—mine is called Bad-Attitude Betty—that tells you to give up, sometimes before you even start. Truth is, distractions abound, no matter how well we've set ourselves up to avoid them. Sure, they look different for each one of us, but they are real and they can be spectacularly disruptive.

Naturally, this is where our brains start to launch a campaign against change—when we don't yet have proof it will be a worthwhile experiment. Remember from an earlier chapter that 40% to 45% of our daily activities are actually habits, including things like what time we rise in the morning and how we spend our time once we do. To the inevitable question of "What's the worst that can happen?" with a

5 a.m. alarm and 4% fix plan, your brain may, in fact, have a variety of solid responses:

- **I'll be exhausted.** This is likely the number one argument for not getting up with the other morning larks, and it may end up being true, especially for the first few mornings. But you already know the solution: get to bed earlier.

- **I'll wake up early but make no progress.** Yes, that would suck. And yes, you should expect it to happen. While you may view it as losing a precious hour with your comfy mattress, you could flip things around to see it as building a foundation. You are beginning to reshape your morning habits, and it won't all fall into place on day one.

- **I'll get on a roll and then something will put me off course.** Otherwise known as "Is there any point of starting if I can't be sure I'll finish?" The answer is always HELL YES. Also, things *will* happen to derail your progress. That's a given. Count on it the way you would the rising and setting of the sun, then get over it.

- **I'm not ready to uproot my current habits.** This is perhaps the most honest assessment. Change is awkward. It can also be downright unpleasant, and who wants to make life feel harder than it already does? What this really comes down to is your level of commitment—to yourself. If

Groundhog Day is working for you, great. But if not, try giving yourself that first slice of cake before anyone else gets a piece. It doesn't get any simpler (or more complicated, because again, change is hard) than that. Great news, right?

The point is, experimentation involves some risk. The thing you planned for doesn't always come to fruition, even with the best intentions. All of which *can* lead to a sense of failure . . . but that's no reason to stop trying! Consider a few famous examples of failed experiments that eventually led to great outcomes:

- **WD-40:** This useful product is a household lifesaver, but did you know it got its name because there were 39 failed attempts at creating a degreaser and rust protection solvent before success happened on try number 40? It was originally designed for the aerospace industry, but it became so popular with employees, it was packaged and sold in aerosol cans in 1958.

- **Dyson vacuums:** While these vacuums are a top seller today, founder James Dyson apparently tested 5,271 prototypes before finally creating a vacuum that worked. However, the trouble wasn't over, as he couldn't find a company to license and manufacture his vacuum, so he started his own manufacturing operation. It was a risk that paid off: James Dyson is now worth $6.2 billion.

- **Bubble wrap:** This was originally created in 1960 as a trendy textured wallpaper, and needless to say, it wasn't a hit. Later, an attempt to use it as housing insulation also failed. Finally, IBM used the product to package its newly launched computer, and bubble wrap became the huge success it is today.

So let's approach "what's the worst that can happen?" from our new perspective. Experimentation can lead to unexpected, wonderful things, and getting up early to capture a just-for-you hour at the start of your day is a great way to test this hypothesis. That doesn't mean you shouldn't set a specific goal. You should, because if you don't, you may find yourself doing everything but the one thing you hoped to focus on.

But as clichéd as it sounds, the journey here really is as important as the final destination. Learning to speak Italian fluently enough to engage in a meaningful conversation may be what you're going for, but being able to ask where the washroom is if you're on vacation in Italy should also be considered a success. Little wins can be as satisfying as big ones, as long as you frame them as such.

TRUST THE PROCESS

When you doubt your power, you give power to your doubt.
—Honoré de Balzac

"You can do better."

This was how a letter—written to me by a reader, on fancy stationery, and mailed old-school to my publisher—ended. Four simple words. The woman's name was Marlene, and she was quite disappointed in me and my book (my sophomore novel). So much so that she went to the trouble to write a detailed letter, typing it out in a terse font on decorative stationery, before tracking me down via my publisher's address and popping said letter in the mail.

What had I done in my book to make Marlene so upset? I had used a word she found "offensive." She never said exactly what the word was, but she quite clearly stated she found it vulgar and unnecessary. I can only guess which word she was referring to, and I assume it's the one that starts with an *f* and rhymes with "duck." Regardless, Marlene went on to say she had been quite enjoying the novel before she came across "that word" but then she refused to continue reading. At the end of her letter she added: ". . . being that you're an author, I imagine you have an excellent handle on language, and therefore *you can do better*."

Some authors might have been put off by this. But I loved getting that letter and promptly shared it with my closest writer friends, who commiserated and chuckled (these sorts of letters are part of being an author) but who also gave Marlene props for her conviction and effort. And from there the mantra "You can do better" was born, and it's one we continue to use—tongue-in-cheek—to this day.

While Marlene's declaration rolled off my back, she's not the only person who has told me I can do better. In fact, I have told *myself* this very thing, more than once. In the previous chapter I told you that the asshole voice in my head is named Bad-Attitude Betty, but she has a cousin I should perhaps name Marlene. The "You can do better" voice in my head has surfaced at various times of life—for example, when I'm in novice territory or after I've put in much time and effort on something only to realize it won't work out after all. And as expected, this negative internal voice can bring all my creativity and focus to a grinding halt.

The real issue stems from a lack of trust. Specifically, trust in the process, but also in the skills required to do the task at hand. It's all well and good to apply the "Fake it till you make it" mantra when you feel out of your element, but it doesn't make the experience any easier. You still have to *trust* you can do it, even if you aren't exactly sure how. We all deal differently with this challenge; some of us engage supportive friends and family, or even strangers on social media, to hold us accountable, while others prefer to operate in solitary confinement before sharing the details of a project or venture.

My solution to chipping away at the challenge is found close to home, with my husband. He is one of my greatest cheerleaders, including with my writing. He sweetly believes, wholeheartedly, that I deserve every accolade and then some, and is appropriately frustrated on my behalf with the struggles all authors deal with. And while he doesn't read all my novels (he's more of a non-fiction guy), he is always there for me when I need to brainstorm. I typically sit him down at the beginning of every project and ask him, "Where are the holes?" because he is skilled at calling me on my writing hang-ups, but he also has a keen sense for when something isn't quite "there" yet. However, one thing I try to avoid asking him for help with is the premise of the idea itself. Because that often goes something like this:

Me: Okay, so this is about two women, and one has a crazy secret (insert crazy secret) that will completely destroy the other woman's life, and it's a race between the secret coming out and burying it forever.

Husband: Right. Okay. So . . . what if there's some sort of secret code or poison that is carried onto a commercial plane in some regular form, like a pack of gum or something, but then it gets switched somehow and the poison ends up with the wrong guy?

Me: ——

I can't tell you the number of times the above scenario has played out. I laugh when it happens now, though it used to get under my skin and make me doubt what I was doing—because his ideas are usually good ones; they just aren't the right ideas for the types of books I write, or want to write. Such discussions would inevitably lead to a "You can do better, Karma" conversation with myself. Which may be accurate but is not super-helpful at the early stages of a writing project.

What I have learned to do over the years is to trust the process involved in those at-times maddening conversations with my husband. Trust that the reason I go to him *first* is because he gives me just the right amount of pushback before I commit to an idea 100%. This has probably saved me hours of bang-head-against-wall time and is a critical part of my writing process.

After the mildly demoralizing yet useful conversation with my husband, I pull out my desk calendar, my gratitude journal, my copy of Elizabeth Gilbert's *Big Magic*, and my YOU ROCK mug—my arsenal. It's also around when I send desperate texts and emails to dear friends who also have skin in this writing game, with headings like "Mayday, Mayday" and "Marlene Is Back." Because imposter syndrome flare-ups are unpleasant but highly predictable, I trade my fear and worry for an inspirational reminder, which usually goes something like: "This current torment is merely preparation for something great to happen." That may seem hokey, but your mind is amazingly malleable and is always happy to switch to a more positive loop.

If you have an idea for something you want to do but have been talking yourself out of for a while now, it's time to quiet that "You can do better" voice in your head. Banish your own Marlene or Bad-Attitude Betty—that surly character who lives inside all of us—and decide that it's enough already. *Trust the process.*

Whatever you do, don't count yourself out before you've even made the attempt. If I had gone that route, my first novel would be lying half-finished in a dusty drawer. I would not have had the opportunity to write further novels and receive Marlene's letter. Without Marlene, I wouldn't have had the anecdote for this book, which I wouldn't even be writing because I would not be an author and probably would have returned to sleeping in past 5 a.m.

You have no idea what you're capable of until you go for it. And that applies to both the big things and the smaller ones—success and happiness do not live only in huge experiences, but in the tinier ones too.

Trust the process. You can do it.

ONE LAST WORD:
WE ALL SLEEP IN SOMETIMES

Imperfections are not inadequacies;
they are reminders that we're all in this together.
—BRENÉ BROWN

The strangest thing happened as soon as I accepted the offer and signed the contract for this book, which as you now know centred around my experience of getting up at 5 a.m. to find time to write.

I started sleeping in.

The first morning it happened, I figured it was a fluke, because a deeply entrenched habit doesn't just—*poof*—disappear overnight. Yes, it could have been the result of a few later-than-average nights and the need for a teensy bit more shut-eye. I mean, it was only 6:30 a.m., so not exactly late or a sleep-in by others' standards. But then, the next morning, I cruised right past my alarm again, getting out of bed at 7:20 a.m.—definitely "sleeping in" for a typical 5 a.m. morning lark. It was the latest I had slept in for years. Like, *years*.

After it happened a few more times that week, I thought, *Okay, then, here we are, I guess*. That was it: my 5 a.m. wake-up days were behind me. I wondered if I'd finally used them up the way you do a Costco-sized bag of chocolate chips—it seems it will last forever, and you get complacent about always having chocolate chips, but then one day you go to make cookies and discover the bag is empty, save for a scant handful of sad chocolate chips at the bottom.

At this point, I panicked a little. Imposter syndrome kicked in, and I thought, *How can I write a book about getting up at 5 a.m. when I'm not actually waking up at 5 a.m. anymore?* Even my husband casually asked, on one of these late-to-wake mornings, wasn't I worried about writing a book about being a morning lark when I no longer seemed able to wake up early. (Yes, yes, dear husband, I was worried.)

Eventually, after about two weeks of this, my early-to-rise schedule miraculously reverted back. I never figured out what caused me to sleep in, but I am grateful it happened. It reminded me that this whole "get up and get to it" thing isn't like riding a bike—it seems to not be one of those skills that, once you master it, is yours forever. If you find yourself falling off the wagon, the best approach is to give yourself a break and not make a big deal out of it.

I have a good friend who, after much humming and hawing and a series of "Give 5 a.m. a try . . . what's the worst that can happen?" discussions, finally became a morning lark writer. And once she did, she was hooked. Suddenly, she had time and space to focus on her creative self, without the usual interruptions or barriers that can occur later on, as everyone else helps themselves to cake slices until there's nothing left on the plate but a smear of icing. But again, this is a habit-forming behaviour (good news!) that can also be a touch finicky (less good news). This friend coasted along with her 4% fix, waking at 5 a.m. for months, and then the summer hit. And suddenly the drastic shift in her kids' schedules, from structured to a more free-range approach (no school, everyone staying up late, vacations, a general disregard for schedules), meant she was blowing past her 5 a.m. wake-ups every morning. Now, even though her schedule was less demanding in the summer, it didn't mean there wasn't still stuff to do, and so my friend stumbled along, her writing pace going from roadrunner to tortoise. Cue the negative emotions: frustration, disappointment, stress, imposter syndrome. All the while, I reassured her that habits that disappear can be reactivated—science says so! And sure enough, once school was back in session, so were her 5 a.m. creative periods.

It's important to remember that if you decide to try your own 4% fix, your execution will, at times, be imperfect. We are not robots, and this is not a training manual, and things are never as clear-cut as they seem. Most days we're trying to fit round pegs into square holes across a variety of aspects of life.

I've been getting up before the sun for years and have obliterated three laptop keyboards—the keys are scratched off—and have written seven, and counting, books during that time. However, I remain a perpetual learner. I still make the choice to ignore my alarm some mornings. Or I go rogue, ignore my plan, and scroll through Twitter or Instagram for the hour rather than write. There are days when, despite BHAG-level motivation, I'm not even close to reaching my morning's PHAG.

It's all fine. It really is. The 4% fix isn't going anywhere—we may not be able to generate a 25th hour, but the ones we have are here to stay. Because even on those mornings when I don't engage with my first hour the way I hoped, I know things will reset. There will be a freshly baked 24-slice cake available the next morning. And I can try again for that first slice, first thing, as can you.

Hey, we all sleep in sometimes.

RESOURCES:
IN THE INTEREST OF (SAVING) TIME

Finish every day, and be done with it. For manners, and for wise living, it is a vice to remember. You have done what you could—some blunders and absurdities no doubt crept in; forget them as fast as you can. Tomorrow is a new day.
—RALPH WALDO EMERSON

DECIDE *WHY* YOU WANT TO GET UP

Putting aside obvious answers such as a sick kid or an early-morning appointment or a money-making activity, write a list of three to five things that interest you enough that getting up early wouldn't make you angry. Or think about something you've always imagined would be fun and write it down. Or perhaps it's time to reach way back and remember something you used to enjoy but haven't done in a while. *Be specific:* focus on the details of a 4% fix project with the same specificity, for example, that you'd apply to a Starbucks beverage order. (No one walks up to a barista and says, "One coffee, please!") Don't forget, this is not about perfection or productivity. You do you, but make sure you *do* something.

What's worth getting out of bed for?

1. ....
....
....

2. ....
....
....

3. ....
....
....

4. ....
....
....

5. ....
....
....

PLAN YOUR PROJECTS

Start small. Think of a fun project you can tackle in one or two hours, something that sparks your interest or creativity or some other curiosity you have. Maybe you want to try a new recipe, or read through an article you've had book-marked forever (that has nothing to do with work), or walk 5 kilometres with the dog before everyone else is up, or create some art in your bullet journal, or finish that book that has been on your nightstand forever, or make a playlist for your next workout.

Now think of another similar project . . . and then one more. You should have three projects in front of you that can be finished in about the time it takes to get a haircut or to wait in line to get your driver's licence renewed or to grocery shop for a long weekend or to get a dental cleaning (what you record below should be a lot more fun, by the way).

Focus on *fun*, not flawlessness, when deciding on your projects.

So, I got out of bed . . . now what?

1. ....

....

....

2. ....

....

....

3. ....

....

....

GET CREATIVE

Take a few moments and write down how you view your own creativity. Do you identify as creative? If you don't currently see yourself that way, do you wish you did? What does creativity mean to you, and for you? What scares you about the idea of pursuing something creative with a 4% fix hour?

Being creative means . . .

I feel most creative when I'm . . .

Ways in which I would like to practise creativity:

....
....
....
....
....
....

What's holding me back from pursuing a creative project?

....
....
....
....
....
....

CHOOSE YOUR FOCUSED FOUR

What are your daily priorities, the things you *want* to focus your attention on (family, health, spirituality), versus the things that demand your focus (work, errands, responsibilities)? These categories may remain constant, or they can change at whatever frequency works for you.

Category 1:

_____

_____

_____

_____

_____

Category 2:

_____

_____

_____

_____

_____

Category 3:

....

....

....

....

....

....

Category 4:

....

....

....

....

....

....

BE BOLD

What's on your bucket list? Write down 5 to 10 things. They could be anything, from a creative project to countries you want to visit, to a new career you've always been intrigued by, to volunteering with an organization close to your heart, to eating at 10 of the world's best restaurants. You do not have to figure out *how* to do these things at this point—that can, and will, come later. This is a space for dreaming, without restrictions:

One day I hope to . . .

1. ....

....

....

2. ....

....

....

3. ....

....

....

4. ....

....

....

5. ....

....

....

6. ....
....
....

7. ....
....
....

8. ....
....
....

9. ....
....
....

10. ....
....
....

Now that you have the beginnings of a bucket list, it's time to take the first step in tackling it. Choose one thing from the list above—don't stress about logistics—circle it, and set your alarm to wake up a half hour earlier than you normally do. Spend those 30 minutes getting creative about how to achieve that goal.

This is daydreaming in action: imagine the goal, feel the excitement build at the prospect of experiencing the activity and ticking that box, and then write down an actionable strategy for how you're going to start achieving it. Even if it's just a first step, like "Book a babysitter so my significant other and I can talk this idea through" or "Research one destination from my travel bucket list" or "Send an email to the charity I'd like to support, asking about volunteer opportunities." Whatever your goal is, give yourself that first piece of cake by giving this idea 30 minutes of your time.

My "fill the bucket" action plan:

MY 4% FIX—THE FINAL CURTAIN

Don't overthink this part. Be free with your ideas, be bold with your plan, be committed to progress versus perfection, and have fun. Write in (erasable) pencil or indelible ink— it's up to you—but make sure you write something down.

I will remember . . .

....

....

....

I will stay focused on . . .

....

....

....

I am grateful for . . .

....

....

....

Wild card

....

....

....

ACKNOWLEDGMENTS

Trying to write a book without a stellar team behind you is like trying to write a book at 5 a.m. without coffee—impossible, at least for this author. My editor, Brad Wilson, has been cucumber-cool since our first meeting, and I'm thankful for his steadfast belief that I would find a path through these pages. Thanks to the rest of the HarperCollins Canada team, especially Zeena Baybayan, Cory Beatty (who planted the seed), Michael Guy-Haddock, Jaclyn Hodsdon, Neil Wadhwa, Iris Tupholme, and Noelle Zitzer. To Carolyn Forde—without whom I wouldn't even have one book on the shelf, let alone a hefty handful—and the Transatlantic Agency team, thank you, as always.

I had the pleasure of speaking with a number of brilliant people during my research and am appreciative of their time, as well as their wisdom and anecdotes: Gail Vance Civille, Helen Costa-Giles, Lucas Murnaghan, and Brigid Schulte. For my family and friends, I can only do what I do because you all have my back. Thanks especially to my writing coven; my #5amwritersclub crew; the women authors I'm honoured to call friends; and my parents, for the myriad of experiences but also for always giving me a soft place to land. For Adam and Addie, you two put up with a lot, living with an author. I'm fairly sure I owe you *all* the ice cream.

Many of my own experiences were mined to write this book. The moments and anecdotes are as accurate as my memory, so any and all mistakes rest with me. This is a book I never intended to write, but now that I have, thank you for reading. I hope you find your own 4% fix as a result. See you at 5 a.m., friends.